The God Revolution

The God Revolution

A Short Course in Christianity

BRUCE HAMILL

CASCADE *Books* · Eugene, Oregon

THE GOD REVOLUTION
A Short Course in Christianity

Copyright © 2018 Bruce Hamill. All rights reserved. Except for brief quotations in critical publications or reviews, no part of this book may be reproduced in any manner without prior written permission from the publisher. Write: Permissions, Wipf and Stock Publishers, 199 W. 8th Ave., Suite 3, Eugene, OR 97401.

Cascade Books
An Imprint of Wipf and Stock Publishers
199 W. 8th Ave., Suite 3
Eugene, OR 97401

www.wipfandstock.com

PAPERBACK ISBN: 978-1-60608-615-5
HARDCOVER ISBN: 978-1-5326-3260-0
EBOOK ISBN: 978-1-5326-3259-4

Cataloguing-in-Publication data:

Names: Hamill, Bruce, author.

Title: The God revolution : a short course in Christianity / Bruce Hamill.

Description: Eugene, OR : Cascade Books, 2018 | Includes bibliographical references.

Identifiers: ISBN 978-1-60608-615-5 (paperback) | ISBN 978-1-5326-3260-0 (hardcover) | ISBN 978-1-5326-3259-4 (ebook)

Subjects: LCSH: Christianity.

Classification: BR121.2 .H36 2018 (print) | BR121.2 .H36 (ebook)

Manufactured in the U.S.A.   07/19/18

To Jan

Faith is the capacity to put all your eggs in the one basket when even the existence of the basket must be taken on trust and hope.

Hebrews 11:1 [paraphrased by Nathan Nettleton]

If you remove the yoke from among you, the pointing of the finger, the speaking of evil, if you offer your food to the hungry and satisfy the needs of the afflicted, then your light shall rise in the darkness and your gloom be like the noonday.

Isaiah 58:9–10

That pseudo-humanism that calls itself Christianity intends precisely to forbid that anyone be sacrificed.

Friedrich Nietzsche

God does not die on the day we cease to believe in a personal deity, but we die on the day when our lives cease to be illumined by the steady radiance, renewed daily, of a wonder, the source of which is beyond all reason.

Dad Hammarskjold, *Markings*

Contents

List of Illustrations

Preface

THIS BOOK IS WRITTEN for adults or intelligent older teens who don't know much about the Christian faith but are at least partly open to it. It assumes that the reader shares many of the presuppositions of contemporary secular liberal culture in the West. It also assumes that the reader will have some degree of scepticism regarding the truth claims of Christianity and hopefully will not simply assume that if it's "in the bible" then it's true.

The book can be read either individually or as a study guide for a group. To this end I have included questions for discussion along the way.

The plan is to put Christian thought and experience in an historical context and then to invite the serious reader to perhaps visit a Christian community and observe it in action or in worship and to perhaps consider an experiment called "the Christian life." There are no proofs or knock-down arguments, just a fascinating story that I trust will connect with the lives and dilemmas of contemporary readers.

The first chapter is introductory and seeks to engage with some existential questions. The following three chapters can be looked at as having a trinitarian structure—i.e., fitting with the three-fold name of God as Trinity: Father, Son and Spirit. The first concerns the Father (Abba) of Jesus. The second concerns the life, death and resurrection of Jesus. The third looks at the Spirit of Jesus and the work of the Spirit and with that the consequences of Jesus in the community that flows from it and the theory and hope it inspires.

Although there is considerable historical background in each chapter, the reader is invited, in different ways, to read the story from the perspective created by the revolution centered on the resurrection of Jesus. So each chapter is prefaced by two boxed summaries of the contents—one from the temporal perspective of the history of Israel and the Ancient Near East and the other from the perspective of the Christian believer. I contend that these two stories are not mutually exclusive. The reader need not remain in the non-committal stance of the student of history and can choose to enter imaginatively into the latter perspective as well. It is the hope of the book that the reader does make that journey.

Acknowledgments

I AM GRATEFUL TO my old Dunedin parish, Coastal Unity, for the support that enabled me to take Study Leave and work on this book and for the Young Adults group who reminded me how hard it is to find good introductory material on Christianity.

Thanks also to the many friends who either encouraged me to undertake the project or who took the time to read and comment on drafts of this book.

In particular thanks to:

Andrew Shepherd, André Muller, Murray Rae, Jonathan Boston, Sonya Lewthwaite, Jon Screech, Derek Woodard-Lehman, Ben Hudson, Paul Barber, Phil Fountain, Jason Goroncy, Jillian Criglington, Paul Prestidge.

Special thanks also to Janet Weir who kindly offered art for cause.

Most of all thanks to Jan has lived through the days when the book has dominated my mind and our lives.

Introduction

Everything should be made as simple as possible, but not simpler.—ALBERT EINSTEIN

WHY A COURSE IN Christianity?

Because it's interesting.

And because Christianity is in big trouble.

In New Zealand more people claim "no religion" than some form of Christianity. The "nones" have it. What's more a lot of bullshit is going down in the name of Christianity. If you are a two-parent family and both parents are "committed Christians" your statistical probability of passing on the faith is about 50 percent. So maybe a fresh approach might be helpful.

Because the church is facing a crisis of confidence in its central message.

Because most people under the age of fifty now have very little understanding of the basics of Christianity.

Christianity is clearly an enormously large topic. It is a diverse global movement which has shaped nearly everything about the modern world. It is a monstrosity! Introducing all of twenty-first-century Christianity is well beyond the scope of this book.

This book has a much narrower focus. It is an introduction to the thing that got Christianity going in the first place and continues to make it interesting. All it will try to do is provide enough of a sense of what it is all about, how it arose historically and what it might mean for us today to tempt people to explore further.

If you are burnt out on Christianity this book may interest you, but you are not the primary intended audience. There are many books written to re-ignite interest among those who have given up on Christianity as they know it. This one is written for those who are largely unfamiliar with Christianity and don't have much prior background and language.

This introduction will not provide extensive historical or scholarly information. Nor will it treat Christianity as a kind of philosophy that can be reduced to a set of formulae that answer questions no one is asking.

For all its diversity, Christianity has a central simplicity. It is first of all a way of doing life and, in turn, a way of thinking about life. We will look at historical information and even a bit of philosophy along the way, but in the end the invitation of this course is to experiment with a way of life and thought.

So if your motivation to look at Christianity is one of curiosity be aware—or beware!—you can't really understand Christianity like some interesting artefact to be put under the microscope. Christianity is like swimming. You have to jump in the water. The real reason for taking up this challenge is not *simply* "because it's interesting." In the end it has to be because it matters, and because how we live our lives matters. So let's get down to the core questions.

What Is a Christian?

A Christian is a follower of Jesus. At least that's the short answer. Following Jesus is a way of life. To be a Christian is not really a status thing, it's something you do. If someone asks you *how* to become a Christian as if being a Christian were a status you might achieve, in order to qualify for something, then they are confused. The correct answer to their question is simply "follow Jesus." Being a Christian and becoming a Christian amount to the same thing. Not that following Jesus is necessarily simple; nor is it obvious what it means to follow Jesus, but the point is, you don't do something *in order to* become a follower, you just follow. If your concern is to qualify for something or to be rewarded with some status, like a reserved seat in heaven, then you are probably not following Jesus. Such motivation undermines the point of it all, since following Jesus involves letting go of such self-interest and ambition.

All definitions can be confusing and can create misunderstanding. We need a fuller answer. Here's a slightly expanded version:

A Christian is a person who follows Jesus,

empowered by the Spirit of God,

as if their life depended on it.

In other words, following Jesus is not just a hobby. It's a God thing. It takes seriously the challenge of living life as if it mattered in a more than trivial sense.

To be a Christian, to jump into the experiment of the Christian life, is to find oneself in the middle of a puzzle—not merely an intellectual puzzle but also a life puzzle, a puzzle about Jesus, and a puzzle about the mystery of life. Hopefully those who enter into the challenge that Christianity creates will discover something worth dying for and thus worth living for. To be truly alive you have to die. Hopefully by the end of this book you will have some sense of what that means.

Like all good questions and answers, the one about what a Christian is demands that we go deeper and ask more questions.

So if Christianity is about following Jesus:

- Who is Jesus?
- Why follow anyone in the first place? Isn't it better to be a leader than a follower?
- What's involved in following Jesus rather than just being interested in him?

As for the Spirit of God empowering us:

- What is the Spirit? Is it just another name for God or something different?
- Why do we need power? Can't we just do it ourselves?
- Is this some kind of "superpower"?
- What does the Spirit of God do?

As if my life depends on it:

- Isn't that a bit heavy?
- Why should our life depend on anything other than physical laws?
- What does my life depend on?
- Is it *only* my life that depends on this or do the lives of other people or creatures?
- What happens to me if I don't follow Jesus? If my life depends on it will I die if I don't?

Each of these questions relates to the threefold name for God. They are questions about Jesus, and about the Spirit, and about the God whom Jesus called Abba. They are all closely connected. Hopefully this will be a little bit clearer by the end of this book.

We will follow this structure in the book. We will start with the God question more broadly and historically. This will introduce us to the main issue: Who is Jesus and why is he followed? Finally we will look at things that flow from Jesus and following him—things that have to do with the Spirit of God and the church and what it might mean to have hope for the future.

At the end we will ask these questions again and see if we have made any progress. But before we do any of this let's stay with the question of *dependence* a little longer.

What does my life depend on?

The eternal mystery of the world is its comprehensibility.—
ALBERT EINSTEIN[1]

In this section we will reflect on the question of dependence and what ultimately matters.

If you are reading this book then there is a good chance that you are not an atheist. But we will not take that for granted.

In the end *why* does your life matter? At risk of over simplifying things, it more or less boils down to two views. The first view could be called the *physicalist* view and the latter might be called the *theological* view because it requires something like the existence of God.

> "Jesus is God's Word, God's idea of God, how God understands himself. He is how-God-understands-himself become a part of our human history, become human, become the *first* really thoroughly human part of our history—and therefore of course, the one hated, despised and destroyed by the rest of us, who wouldn't mind being divine but are very frightened of being human."
>
> —HERBERT MCCABE[2]

Why does my life matter according to the first view?

It matters because it matters *to me* . . . and it matters to me basically because I don't want to die. It matters to me as a simple result of my drive to survive in the world and not die. It matters because my genes (Richard Dawkins says we have "selfish genes"[3]) have programmed me to avoid dying. So when I am in danger I instinctively follow one of three options: flight, fight, or freeze. For life to matter is for death to be a threat. As long as I can maintain certain biological processes I am alive and that is all that matters, certainly what matters above all else. On this view the thing my life depends on is no more than certain biological

1. Einstein, "Physics and Reality", 64
2. McCabe, *God Still Matters*, 104
3. See Dawkins, *The Selfish Gene*.

processes . . . because after all that's all my life is. This is why we might call it the *physicalist* view.

Alternatively, on the second view, life is *more* than just staying alive and not dying. There is a quality of life that matters as well and not just because I like it. It also matters because it is going somewhere, part of something greater, has a purpose. In contrast to the previous view, dying does not define life. Life is an *achievement* beyond merely maintaining biological processes for as long as possible. It might be possible to keep the biological processes of life functioning and yet fail to be truly alive in this larger sense. And that matters!

But why is there more to life than just not dying? Is there really such a thing as the "good life" or the "true life" or the "beautiful life"? Why?

Some might acknowledge, or want to acknowledge the existence of such things but respond that there *just is*, we don't know why.

Others would say there is more because the world is the creation of and the expression of God who gives it existence and purpose. A world that matters, not merely to me, but regardless of whether it matters to any human being, is better explained by God whose reality is "higher" than our life.

Reality, they would say, is textured with depth and height and a dimensionality that simply cannot be flattened purely to a physicalist level.

Why would we think we might be able to explain or understand the mystery in which our life might potentially have meaning? Perhaps we should stop now. Perhaps the world is too full of shit for such talk. I would simply suggest that before we stop we need to know something about the experience and explanations that have formed the largest religious movement in the world before we give up in advance.

"Keep two pieces of paper in your pockets at all times. One that says 'I am a speck of dust' and the other, 'The world was created for me'"—RABBI BUNIM OF P'SHISHKA

If I were to offer one reason (or possibly three reasons bound together as one) to suggest that this enterprise was worth your time I would say that at least three aspects of our lives cry out for some higher reality: (1) our sense of right and wrong, good and bad, i.e., *moral thinking*; (2) our sense of what is beautiful, i.e., *aesthetic thinking*; and (3) our notion of truth, i.e., *philosophical thinking*. Our feelings of moral duty and responsibility cry out for such an explanation. Our sense that beauty has some objective reality in spite of cultural differences doesn't want to go away. The thought that truth is more than a preference nags us. Indeed when we try, we find we have no way of consistently eliminating the notion of truth from our life and thought. It is better that we seek an understanding of our life that makes good sense of this than to live with it not explained at all.

In short: Better to have tried some faith, and perhaps failed, than not to have tried at all.

If life really matters—not merely because I want it to—then perhaps it matters because of God. Therefore God matters.

Better to have tried some faith, and perhaps failed, than not to have tried at all.

Discussion Question

Is it possible that your deepest desires tell you something about reality, or should you be suspicious of them? Why might they be indicative of the truth? Why might you be suspicious of them?

Activities and Resources

Video: Watch the conversation at the link in the footnote between a scholar-priest and a public intellectual about reasons to believe in God and reasons not to.[4]

---

4. ObjectiveBob, "Why believe in God?—Sarah Coakley." https://www.youtube.com/watch?v=w1RBsgOO4lA

Book: Read *Harold and the Purple Crayon* by Crockett Johnson.[5]

Discussion: What does Harold and the Purple Crayon say about our lives? Do you think there is any alternative to the world created by Harold.

---

5. Johnson, *Harold and the Purple Crayon*, 1955. It's available on YouTube here: https://www.youtube.com/watch?v=ZVaOOgWyvJM.

1

The Sources of the God Revolution

In which a small and frequently oppressed group in the Ancient Near East[1] tells disturbing stories about "God" that reframe the world and their moral imagination, setting the scene for a big break with paganism.[2]

or

In which the creator of the universe takes the time to capture the imagination and life of a small and often persecuted group in the Ancient Near East in order to save the world from a perverted form of human life.

Introduction: Reading the Old Testament

God said to Moses: "I am He who is."[3] *(Exodus 3:14)*

THE CHRISTIAN IDEA OF God has a history. Unsurprisingly, it didn't just always exist. But more than that, the history of "God"

---

1. The ancient Near East was the home of early civilizations within a region roughly corresponding to the modern Middle East. Cf. https://en.wikipedia.org/wiki/Ancient_Near_East.

2. Paganism was (until the twentieth century) a term used by Christians to refer to other religions, usually those with many deities. Only recently have some groups begun to refer to themselves as pagan.

3. This is my own translation.

hinges on a revolutionary moment that is not just a revolution in ideas but an "earthquake" in the shape of human life itself.

To explore this claim requires of us a little of an old-fashioned virtue, humility. We need to be open to the possibility that in spite of our modern scientific sophistication and deeply engrained sense of moral superiority we might just have something in common with the ancient world and even might be able to learn something from them.

The most obvious way to understand the history of "God" is to read the Bible. Unfortunately it is very long and has some *really* boring bits that often stop people getting right through it. The main problem many people have is that they don't understand the background and because the text is so ancient this makes it hard to understand (and easy to misunderstand!). Even though there are important threads holding it together, the Bible is more like an ancient library than a single book. For our purposes in this section we need to get some idea of the first part of the Bible—the Old Testament (or Hebrew Scriptures). The basic reason is quite simple. The Old Testament records the sources of this "God Revolution" we are exploring.

Jesus, Christianity contends, is the center of the God revolution, and he drew his understanding from the Old Testament. Jesus was a Jew. He believed that God was at work in the history of his people as recorded in the books of the Hebrew Scriptures. However he was not a fundamentalist.[4] He had his own unique, selective and critical take on these historical sacred writings. He didn't just take it all as equally authoritative. In what follows we will give some historical background to the Old Testament and give a selective overview of the highlights. It will certainly not be exhaustive—more like a teaser to introduce us to how Jesus fits in.

As well as being a whole library of books, the Old Testament is diverse. It is not a single uniform source. In some ways it shows us the *arguments* about God that were going on in the thinking of the Hebrew people. So what you get is a glimpse of a long history

---

4. In this context "fundamentalist" refers to someone who treats their Scriptures as if they were written directly by God.

of thought and debate. We will focus primarily on the sides of those arguments that Jesus took up and the way he transformed the story he inherited. There is both continuity and discontinuity between Jesus and the Hebrew Scriptures. All of these Scriptures are useful, but not always in the same way.

Discussion Question

Does it surprise you that texts might be both "sacred" Scriptures and critically read? What assumptions might make sense of this?

The World in Which Israel Was Born

The God of the Underdogs

The Christian idea of God started life with the name Yahweh, the God of the underdogs. Sometime between 1300 BC and 500 BC—a long time to be sure—something very different emerged in a small people group in the Middle East located along the coast of the Mediterranean on the trade routes between powerful empires like Babylonia, Assyria, and Egypt. A particular distinctive of this people group was that they were regularly brutalized by armies of empires. They were the underdogs of the Ancient Near East. The fact that they were the underdogs is not accidental to the story and vision of life that emerged. However, this vision is only interesting if you understand what it came out of and what it contrasted with. If Jewish faith was that different, what was it different from?

Sacrifice: Ancient Economics

If there is any common factor in ancient culture across the globe it is the presence of some form of sacrificial ritual (or cult). The Ancient Near East is no exception. It was not really what we would call "religion" but more like economics. Sacrifice was the focus around which they organized their life. There was no such thing as "private religion" in the ancient world. Sacrifice was basically the way communities together did deals with the gods. What we nowadays might think of as natural force, forces outside of human control, were believed to be in the control of more powerful beings. Life was maintained by negotiating with these higher beings. The logic of this system has been described as *do ut des*—a Latin phrase meaning "I give in order to receive."

For further exploration of this theme you might like to check out Mel Gibson's movie *Apocalypto* as a source of reflection on sacrificial culture, as well as Bishop Robert Barron's commentary at the link in the footnote.[5]

A Violent Cosmos

However, this system of exchange (i.e., giving sacrifices of human or animal or crop to the gods to gain security or prosperity) was more deeply linked to the problem of violence. It was linked to violence both in the way the ancients thought about the world and in the way they dealt with it. Their view of the world assumed that the universe itself was in a state of conflict or struggle. Conflict in human life was reflected in conflict with and between the gods. The creation stories in the Ancient Near East are usually stories of violence among gods, in which humans are seen as pawns of higher, malevolent powers.

Sacrifice: The Glue That Holds Society Together?

Alongside the common philosophical idea of the cosmos as a struggle, the main common cultural phenomenon of the Ancient Near East was the practice and culture of sacrifice. If social anthropologist René Girard is right, then this too is related to

---

5. Bishop Robert Barron, "Bishop Barron on 'Apocalypto.'" https://www.youtube.com/watch?v=FMoblhmRLKY.

violence, not philosophically but practically. Ancient "religion" (i.e., sacrifice) is not so much a product of trying to imagine the nature of the universe as it is a product of a long history of finding a mysterious peace and unity in the practice of scapegoating someone (i.e., blaming and inflicting violence on one for the problems of the many). In other words, sacrifice had a practical function in controlling violence between human beings and keeping society together. Girard says that sacrificial ritual is a re-enactment of violent acts of scapegoating. The all-against-one structure of the scapegoating process in, for example, a mob lynching, is replicated in the ritual of the sacrifice. So it is worth taking a few moments here to look at this influential way of understanding the ancient world.

Girard claims that the emergence of distinctively human society took a big step forward when it was discovered, over millennia, that blaming—and eliminating—one person produced a common sense of solidarity.

Humans, given the development of their brains, are more profoundly shaped by their fellow creatures than any other animal. This means that the common desires that spread throughout human populations tend to produce greater conflict over the things everyone wants. Girard thinks that the solution to the escalation of conflict is achieved when attention is turned to a common individual/scapegoat, who becomes the victim of the mob, and miraculously—to all appearances—brings peace to the community united against him or her. The one regarded as the problem is suddenly imbued with "sacred" power. Girard posits that sacrificial rituals are re-enactment dramas that reinforce this experience of social unity even after the practice of human sacrifice is replaced with animals or produce.

In short, because of our tendency towards violence, the survival of the human population has depended on a mechanism for controlling this violence. The scapegoating mechanism provides the way in which social unity is achieved by controlling violence with violence. The ancient practice of sacrifice, Girard says, is the outcome of a process that works largely unconsciously to produce what we—sometimes with a note of irony—call civilization. This is why sacrifice is so universal.

I think there is something in this theory. It suggests links between the struggle of human co-existence and our sense of the whole—focussed on this word, "god." According to Girard, the belief that people had in the ancient gods did not arise from sitting around thinking about the cosmos. Rather this conception of the gods arose as a result of a human dynamic and the need to manage intra-human violence. In other words, the ancient god-concepts are the product of scapegoating and sacrifice rather than the other way round.

What If Jewish Faith Is an Alternative to the Violence?

If there is truth in this theory then it is significant background to the Old Testament. Jewish faith as we see it in the Old Testament is not just concerned with the character of God (vs. the gods). It is also thoroughly concerned with the problem of violence and whether there can be an alternative to the sacrificial cultures of the world in which they lived. It is the great alternative of the ancient world, both in terms of cosmology and ethics.

We might conclude, then, that how sacrifice actually works to maintain the unity of human society, and what people think they are doing when they sacrifice to the gods, are not necessarily the same thing. What people thought they were doing was negotiating with the powers of the universe for their survival. For them the wider cosmos was imagined to be a kind of reflection of the human condition. The gods, for all their mystique, were still a part of the world. Their anger needed to be appeased. They needed to be pacified and enlisted in support of the local community. No one asked philosophical questions like "what is a god?"—at least not until philosophy got started. Gods just did stuff. They were part of the way the world worked. In some ways, Yahweh, the God of the Hebrews (I will use a capital G for this new development), started off similarly. However the stuff that God did and the way God did it turned out to be both unique and revolutionary.

We will come back to this in more detail soon, but for now we will move on from a general cultural background to a very brief sketch of the history of Israel as a background to the Old Testament

A Brief History of Israel and the New God

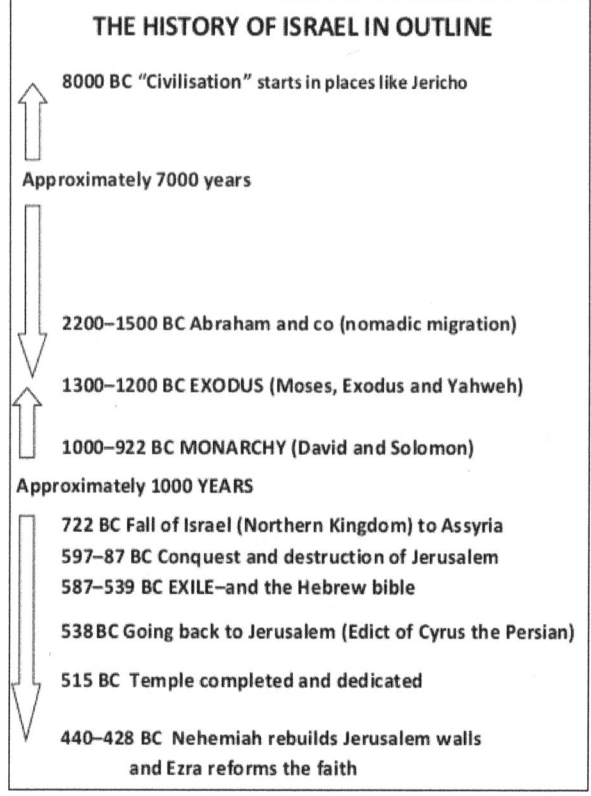

THE HISTORY OF ISRAEL IN OUTLINE

8000 BC "Civilisation" starts in places like Jericho

Approximately 7000 years

2200–1500 BC Abraham and co (nomadic migration)

1300–1200 BC EXODUS (Moses, Exodus and Yahweh)

1000–922 BC MONARCHY (David and Solomon)

Approximately 1000 YEARS

722 BC Fall of Israel (Northern Kingdom) to Assyria
597–87 BC Conquest and destruction of Jerusalem
587–539 BC EXILE–and the Hebrew bible

538 BC Going back to Jerusalem (Edict of Cyrus the Persian)

515 BC Temple completed and dedicated

440–428 BC Nehemiah rebuilds Jerusalem walls
and Ezra reforms the faith

This seems like a long time ago. But it's a much longer time from the dawn of "civilization" to the establishment of Israel as a distinct people. We might say that human society was already old by then. The story we have to tell fits in the space of a millennium. Historical details are, however, quite hard to pin down accurately. This comes with the nature of the documents we have and the limitations of archaeology. In the end historical details are not very important. Nevertheless, to give a broad context, here is a summary.

Migration and Patriarchs

As best we can tell, the ancestors of the Jewish people were nomadic people from around 2000 BC and following. This context helps to make sense of the story of Abraham. Around 1300 BC a group of nomadic slaves escaped from Egyptian control and with the help of local "apiru" (Hebrews) managed to conquer some city-states and establish themselves in a confederation of tribes. This "exodus" is associated with the name of Moses, and stories are told about it in the Old Testament book entitled Exodus. They shared a loyalty to the god, Yahweh. This is really the beginning of Israel. The cultural practices of life and worship along with the moral code we know as the "Ten Commandments" provided a kind of constitutional basis for the people and were developed at this time.

Exodus, Yahweh, and "Monotheism"

Something like monotheism—belief in only one god—was not completely unheard of in the ancient world. A form of it seemed to have existed in Egypt not long before the great escape—the Exodus. However, while the reduction in the number of gods in Israel (the move from polytheism towards monotheism) is interesting, of even more interest is the change in the meaning of the term "god" and what such a change might imply for human life. It is hard to pin-point when these changes came about since we only know about them via the stories that were gathered and written about 700 years later at a time of crisis for Israel known as the Exile (600–500 BC). Although it looks as if Hebrew ideas emerged in a distinctive way during the time of the Exodus and the conquest of Palestine (1300–1200 BC), they were decisively shaped into the form we now know during this period of exile.

Monarchy

Politically, the high point in the timeline of Israel comes in between these two events with the Monarchy. For a brief moment in history, about a hundred years, Israel was as powerful as any other nation. This moment of national glory with a king, David, and a capital city, Jerusalem, had an enormous impact on Hebrew thinking about God. *Now* the God, Yahweh, who had formed a covenant[6] (agreement) and given Israel a moral code (The Ten Commandments) in the wilderness, was thought to have chosen them to be a nation with a king.

The Prophetic Movement

In the history of faith, the two historical moments—Exodus and Monarchy—produced enormous creative tension in the cultural thinking of Israelites. A group known as "prophets" represented this tension. They stood alongside the monarchy and the temple, seeking to understand both in the light of the original vision of what it meant to worship Yahweh. They were the public intellectuals who asked different and provocative questions like "What is Yahweh doing?" and "Why are you abandoning the way of Yahweh?" On the one hand they stood for Yahweh's demand that they offer him exclusive allegiance and, among other things, not kill one another. On the other hand, there was a sense that the political realities of kingdom and life among empires, often requiring organized violence and warfare, were also a result of Yahweh's covenant with David.

From a modern point of view these questions might seem somewhat trivial if Yahweh were merely the tribal deity of some ancient people. However, if something deeper is going on it will be another matter. Indeed Christians believe, in retrospect, that the truth about God and life has deep connections with these struggles of the prophets.

---

6. A covenant in the ancient near east was a binding promissory commitment, sometimes made unilaterally by a king and sometimes as a formal agreement between nations.

Exile

Around 600 BC the Babylonians destroyed Israel, slaughtered most of the people, burned the cities and Jerusalem to the ground and took the rulers and elite citizens off to Babylon—modern day Baghdad—thousands of miles away, as prisoners in exile.

At this point Israel as an independent entity disappeared. However, the faith and the identity of the Jewish people did not. The prophetic and priestly thinkers carried with them both their cultural memories and also many questions. Exile was the crisis point—a holocaust[7] even—in which the God revolution began to take its classic shape.

Gathering and Writing a Bible

The prophets and priests who gathered in Babylon during the Exile had with them a range of priestly and legal writings as well as two major strands of tradition and storytelling about the origin of Israel. One strand included the large chunks of "beginning stories" and patriarch stories—Abraham through Joseph—of Genesis. The other strand of tradition included the Exodus and invasion stories associated with Moses and onwards. These traditions appear to have been merged at this time into one story to become the raw material for the creative reworking of priestly authors.[8] The first five books of the Hebrew Bible[9] became enormously significant for understanding what it meant to be a Jew. They were the "hardcore" essentials of Judaism. These books were put together with the protest writings of prophets and other later writings we call Wisdom literature. As a result we have inherited a collection called the Old Testament or the

---

7. The term holocaust, popularized in the twentieth century, originally meant "burnt offering" or "annihilation."

8. If you wish to explore further recent scholarship on this history you might consult *Farewell to the Yahwist* by Thomas B. Dozeman and Conrad Schmid listed in the bibliography.

9. These books are known collectively by scholars as the Pentateuch.

Hebrew Bible—depending on your perspective—in three main parts (Law, Prophets, Wisdom). Although a lot of the writing and gathering happened during and after the Exile, it wasn't officially decided what was going to make it into the sacred collection until some time after Jesus died in the first century AD.

Going Inside the Old Testament

An Alternative Creation Story

Enough history for now. As we suggested earlier, in the Hebrew Bible we find two major themes to explore: (1) the problem of violence; and (2) a new conception of God. As we will show, these themes are related.

Read Genesis 1

In pride of place in the Hebrew Bible is a creation story. Creation stories were commonplace in the ancient world. They were a way of thinking and talking about the meaning of the world around them. The Hebrew one makes a stark contrast to the standard pagan creation story. If you haven't read it check out the first creation story in Genesis chapter 1 (there's another one in Genesis chapter 2). It is written by a priest in exile in Babylon. What is interesting is to understand how different it is from a typical creation story of the time. In the Babylonian story of creation—the *Enûma Eliš*—the world emerges as a result of a struggle among the gods. Marduk defeats Tiamat, a god representing the sea, and rips her body in half to create the earth and the skies.

In contrast the Genesis story has only a singular God from whose word all creation—i.e., everything that is not God—comes into existence. There is no struggle. The world is freely given its existence. "And God said, 'Let there be . . . and God saw that it was good" (cf., Gen 1:3-4 and following). The world is given its own process of flourishing. The earth in turn has its own kind of creativity ("Let the earth put forth vegetation . . . ") and human beings are given responsibility to care for the creation.[10] Like the rest of creation they are to be fruitful. In this story of primal peace, God can rest and so can God's creatures.

A "god" of a Different Order

The Hebrew God, here, is completely beyond rivalry with the created world to which he gives life. God exists independently of creation and does not need it or anything else. God nevertheless graciously gives it existence, and all creation depends on God who does so. Such a "god"—i.e., God—cannot have any competitors. It makes absolutely no sense to imagine God being threatened in any way by creation. What matters for these Hebrew thinkers is that God is of a different kind and category from all other so-called gods—both as sole creator of all and as supreme governor of all. If Yahweh is the God who does these things, there can be no other gods . . . or rather, any other gods exist in a completely different category to the creator God, Yahweh. To highlight this difference, later thinkers have described this image of creation as "creation out of nothing"—sometimes in Latin, *creatio ex nihilo*. On this peaceful vision there is nothing over against God with which God must work or struggle in order to create. God alone brings the cosmos into being.

For Further Reflection

A contemporary hymn writer, Kim Fabricius, offers the following imaginative exploration of what it means to think of the world as "creation" in our time.

> Out of nothing God created
> all the somethings that exist;
> from a Bang the world inflated,
> light-years later earth he kissed.

10. Again this is a stark contrast to *Enûma Eliš* where humans are "slaves" to serve malevolent gods.

Starting with the smallest microbe,
    moving from the sea to land,
life evolved around the new globe,
    gently pushed by God's good hand.

"Go!" said God, and animated,
    species spread by law and chance;
Spirit fashioned and related
    each to all in sacred dance.
All that breathes is love's location,
    not just humans in their pride;
by selection and mutation,
    ask the beasts how God can guide.

Now creation groans and shudders,
    plundered, poisoned, colonized
by a beastly little brother,
    self-styled as the one who's wise.
Will the sparrows finally perish,
    though God clothes them and protects?
Time is short, so let us cherish
    all that God will resurrect.[11]

The Problem of Violence Addressed in Genesis

If the world is created in peace, how then do we account for the
violence of humanity? This is not exactly the way the Old Testament
approaches its story. The general term it uses for a failure to live in
God's world and in relation to God is "sin." However when we look at
what that failure looks like in practice it very quickly becomes clear
that it is about a *violation* of relations with human beings and the
created order—a violation whose epitomy is murder. For example,
the Ten Commandments list an ordered progression of such failures
that leads from covetousness[12]—wanting what your neighbor has or
wants—through lying and stealing to murder.

11. Fabricius, "Out of Nothing God Created" in *Paddling by the Shore*, 10.

12. In Hebrew lists the first and last items traditionally have greatest significance. The Ten Commandments is no exception. The last commandment

The Ten Commandments

(Ten Words that describe the life of the people of Yahweh)[13]

1. I am Yahweh your God, who liberated you from slavery; you shall have no other gods before me.

2. You shall not make for yourself an idol or worship an image of anything in creation.

3. You shall not misuse the name of Yahweh your God.

4. Remember to rest every seventh day on the Sabbath—a different day set aside according to the pattern set in the story of God's creation.

5. Honor your father and mother, so that you will live long in the land God has given you.

6. You shall not kill.

7. You shall not commit adultery.

8. You shall not steal.

9. You shall not lie against your neighbor and fellow citizens.

10. You shall not want what belongs to your neighbor and fellow citizens.

In other words, what the Bible calls sins are not an arbitrary list of offenses defined by an arbitrary divine will. They imply an understanding of how violence works against humanity and against

---

is a concise expression of the kind of *mimesis* that produces violence. To covet means to want what the neighbor has or desires. In this light we can see it as the epitome of a failure of loyalty to the peaceful and transcendent God of the first commandment. Thus the commandments that lead up to the last commandment, when read as a progression inwards from the outer frame (i.e., in reverse order), express increasing levels of destruction flowing from the fundamental flaw in relation to God and neighbor—from coveting to false witness to stealing to adultery to killing. For more on this, see Girard, *I See Satan Fall Like Lightning*, 7–16.

13. This is my paraphrase of the Ten Commandments.

the flourishing of creation. A failure to order ourselves rightly towards God—the first commandment—goes with a life shaped by violence. In what follows we will explore how these levels of violence and rivalry make up the theme of the stories of Genesis.

Discussion Question

How might the prominent placement of covetousness (see footnote 12)—wanting what our neighbor has—address our contemporary life?

In Genesis chapter 2 we see that violence arises from a distorted view of God—a god conceived in our image. As the story tells it, the first humans inhabit a garden in which God has instructed them not to eat the fruit of a certain tree—provocatively called, in Genesis 2:9, "the tree of the knowledge of good and evil." A mysterious creature—usually translated "serpent"—suggests that God is anxious about his creatures and is lying to them in order to preserve privileges for himself. "You shall not die, for God knows that when you eat of it your eyes will be opened and you will be like God, knowing good and evil" (Genesis 3:4–5). This lie suggests to Adam and Eve, representatives of humanity, that God (capital G) might be merely a pagan god (small g) and sets humanity against God whom they now imagine to be their rival. This creates the environment of fear that in turn sets the human creatures in rivalry with one another—Adam against Eve and so on.

In these stories of beginnings we see both the struggle for Israel's distinctive vision in the light of the surrounding cultures as well as a fascinating account of how this might relate to the perennial question of the roots of human violence.

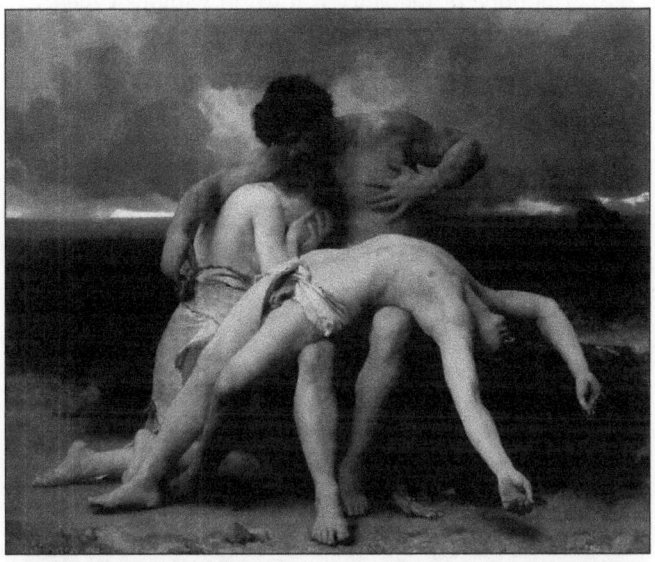

As the story of Genesis continues, sibling rivalry progresses to the famous "first murder" (Cain and Abel). God, however, does not kill Cain, as if God were bound to vengeful justice, but puts a mark on him for his protection to prevent the cycles of revenge: "your brother's blood is crying out to me from the ground" (Genesis 4:10). However, in spite of this, violence escalates and a character called Lamech declares to his wives "I have killed a man for wounding me, a young man for striking me. If Cain is avenged seven-fold, truly Lamech seventy-seven fold" (Genesis 4:23–4). By chapter 6 we read that "the earth was filled with violence" (Genesis 6:11) and God decides to wipe out the human race and start again.

The point of this genocidal story, although it may not seem clear to modern readers, is to continue to find a way beyond violence, and establish human life on a peaceful relationship with God and one another. After the flood God repents and vows never again to act in this manner towards humanity. He warns the survivors that all flesh is sacred. Indeed to combat our tendency to shed one another's blood God reiterates a theme of the creation story, namely that every human being is created in the image of the creator (Genesis 9:6). The hope of the story is a world without violence. The Hebrews call this harmonious world "shalom."

A Story about Organized Violence

Read Genesis 11:1–9

The next story in the Old Testament moves beyond interpersonal violence (epitomized by murder) to violence at the level of social order. The story of the Tower of Babel is a critique of empire. The name Babel is a reference to Babylon—the empire with the famous

Ziggurat. Babel is condemned as a social order without God, a people reaching to the heavens "making a name for themselves" (Genesis 11:4). God's response to this monolithic system of control—the violence of empire—is to confuse it by throwing a spanner in the workings of the single-language system and replacing it with many languages. According to this story it looks as if God is particularly fond of cultural diversity even if it is less efficient.

Discussion Question

How might this story relate to contemporary examples of empire and our struggles with diversity?

A Story about Scapegoating and Forgiveness

Read Genesis 37:1-28, 45:1-5

This series of stories about violence concludes with a story about forgiveness. It follows not only stories about violence, but about sibling rivalry in particular: Cain and Abel; Abraham and Lot; Jacob and Esau; Leah and Rachel. Even Adam and Eve, given their equal status in the garden can be seen as primordial siblings. The story of Joseph explores this dynamic in even more detail than any story thus far, we might even say with a depth rivalling anything in human literature. Here many siblings join forces against the one who stands out. Where the story is particularly complex is where it addresses the steps required to overcome the resentment and alienation and to restore relations among equals. It sets the scene for the theme of forgiveness in the Bible.

Discussion Question

Imagine the feelings of Joseph's brothers who had sold him as a slave years earlier. Where have you experienced the power of forgiveness? What is the message of this ancient story?

As Rabbi Jonathan Sacks[14] says, there is a deep connection in this new Hebrew faith between the mystery of God who, as creator of all, is completely independent of the creation, and the peaceful relations that humanity is called to learn. How we understand the nature of the universe we inhabit and the God who surrounds our life has an enormous impact on how we live it together.

But Isn't the God of the Old Testament Violent?

It is commonly said that the God of the Old Testament is a particularly violent God. There is truth in this claim. You will read a lot of violence in the Old Testament and much of it is attributed God—in this respect there are many similarities with Ancient Near Eastern mythology in general. However, that is only part of the story about the Old Testament. It is helpful to know that the compilers and writers of the *Torah*[15] drew large sections from two distinct and possibly rival traditions about the origins of Israel with different approaches to violence. The situation among Jews on this issue was clearly complex, with diverse views and a lively argument going on. The stories we have looked at so far represent something newly emerging in Hebrew religion. We have focused on these particular stories because we want to explore the roots of Jesus's own view of God and the God revolution he sparked.[16]

14. Jonathan Sacks is a global religious leader, philosopher and author and was from 1991 Chief Rabbi of the United Hebrew Congregations of the Commonwealth.

15. *Torah* is the Hebrew name for the central books of their Scripture. It refers to the first five books (Pentateuch) and is often simply translated "The Law" in English.

16. It is important to be "up front" about the selective nature of this reading of the Old Testament and the reason behind it. There is no point pretending that the collection is uniform. It is a library that documents a debate and dialogue over many years.

A Story about the Nature and Identity of God

Read Exodus 3:1–14

This is another key story for Jewish identity. A particularly fascinating feature is the presence of a bush which burns but is not consumed. God speaks from the bush. In that sense it seems to represent the place of the creator in the world. Some have suggested that it is a symbol for presence of God in the world of God's creation. How can the source of all things exist "in" the creation? Perhaps in a way that neither displaces nor consumes that creation but as its animating and life-giving source—life beyond death.

In response to this experience Moses asks God to identify himself. The answer God gives—using the Hebrew verb to be (YHWH)—can be translated in several ways including "I am the one who is" or "I will be who I will be."

Discussion Question

It is worth taking a moment to discuss or reflect on what the meaning of this strange name might be.

No Image

Rabbi Sacks says that this name is about the Jewish refusal to *image* God. God gives no image or name in the ordinary sense. God retains freedom from us. This is not simply because God is beyond our imagination—that's certainly true. Rather if we do imagine God we cannot help but imagine God *in our own* image. When this happens God becomes like *us* and not like *them*—the other group. In other words we tend to enlist God in our struggles on our side. If, on the other hand, God creates all people as images of God then God's own image can and must be found in the one who is *not in my image. Many images* and *no image* are both about *shalom*—the Hebrew notion of a peaceful life together with the entire created world. In this world each person we encounter has a dignity, value and beauty from the creative work of God. So Hebrew monotheism is not primarily about the difference between one god and many gods. It is about the singular God who is the giver of all life—unconditioned by anything else—and who frees people from slavery and oppression and then summons them communally to practice hospitality to neighbors and strangers.

Resource

If you want to explore this amazing section of the Bible further check out *Not in God's Name* by Chief Rabbi Jonathan Sacks.[17]

Sacrifice in Israel (Upside-Down Sacrifice)

What do you give to someone who has everything and needs nothing? It's the kind of question you might ask yourself at Christmas time if you have rich family members. In a way it is also the key to the changes within Hebrew worship. The Hebrew people were once part of the sacrificial culture of the Ancient Near East. However, with a changing idea of God came changes in their sacrificial religion. It is in the structure of the ritual of the temple that we see signs of the new God.

"For the life of an animal is in the blood, and I [God] have provided the blood for you on the altar to make atonement for your lives; for the blood itself, the life, makes atonement."[18] (Leviticus 17:11)

With the monarchy and the building of a temple came an elaborate expression of the unique Jewish understanding of God. It is in the structure of the routine practices of this temple that we

17. See Sacks, *Not in God's Name*, 107–206

18. This is my translation.

see signs of the new God. We see this in particular in the ritual of "atonement." The Old-English word "at-one-ment" nicely captures the way this ritual is focused on the healing of broken relationships. At this point, where we might expect to see an exchange in which gifts of blood are offered to appease an angry deity (as in Aztec or Mayan religion), we find, instead, what looks like the reverse happening. The blood offering becomes God's gift to the people rather than the people's gift to God. The blood offering—symbolizing life and healing—becomes God's gift to the people rather than the people's gift to God. In Israel's temple the priest who enacts the ritual comes out from the "Holy of Holies"—the place in the middle of the temple symbolizing where God is before creation—wearing the name of Yahweh (YHWH) on his forehead.[19] The priest then brings out the blood of a lamb and comes out into the created world, through a veil made of rich materials symbolizing the riches of creation, and sprinkles the blood for the life and healing of creation. What is important here is that the priest acts *as God*. God is offering life to creation. The lamb is slaughtered and its blood is sprinkled. At the same time a goat—a symbol of Satan and of the sin of the people—is released and sent away. In this way the Hebrew notion of God as creator subverts the logic of pagan sacrifice. God graciously provides the healing that creation needs rather than demands a payment in blood or some other form.

Discussion Questions

It is not hard to see how the human situation needed healing from its relational disorder. How might the Hebrew imagination see the wider creation in need of healing?

Where this really gets worked out is in the exile. The exile prompted profound reflection on suffering. How could Israel's suffering be consistent with the purposes of God? The Old Testament has another story in the book of Job that is a kind of extended parable exploring this issue. Job is portrayed as a good man who

19. See Rapien, *The High Priest as Representative Angel.*

nevertheless suffers and thus tests whether such suffering might be compatible with trust in the goodness of Yahweh.

Second-Isaiah: A New Kind of Hope

From a Christian perspective, the culmination of the Old Testament came with one of the writers of the book of the prophet Isaiah. Scholars call him Second Isaiah. Not only did he inspire Jesus, he was also the first port of call for the writers of the New Testament when they later re-read the Old Testament with fresh eyes. He started to write at the point when the Babylonian Empire was about to be defeated by the Persian ruler Cyrus (circa 540 BC). He writes with great confidence in the redemption[20] of Yahweh. Not only will Yahweh restore Zion—another name for Jerusalem—but Yahweh, through Zion, will restore the world, bringing an end to violence and injustice. Most importantly, this great optimism—better universal hope—is rooted not in a military solution but in suffering. Second Isaiah offers profound exploration of the suffering of Israel and the character of Israel's God. Alongside Zion, the *place* of redemption, the book of Isaiah introduces the *Servant of Yahweh*, an *agent* of redemption, who through his innocent suffering and non-retaliation, acts on behalf of the Lord and brings healing. Because it is so revolutionary it is worth spending some time studying this poem.

Isaiah 52:13—53:12

[13]Look my servant will thrive;

he will be exalted and lifted up to the heights.

[14]Just as there were many who were shocked at him

—his appearance and shape was so damaged
that he didn't look human—

---

20. The term *redemption* has more recently become a common term thanks to its thematization in movies. It originated in the ancient world in the context of economics and meant "buying back," often from slavery. More broadly it refers now to an act that brings good out of a bad situation.

¹⁵so he will startle many nations;

kings will be silent, dumbstruck because of him;

for they shall see what they have never been told before,

and will contemplate things unheard of.

⁵³:¹Who could have believed what we have heard?

And to whom has the work of Yahweh been revealed?

²He grew up before Yahweh like a young plant,

and like a root out of dry ground;

he had no grace or majesty to catch our attention,

nothing desirable in his appearance.

³He was despised and rejected by others;

a suffering man well acquainted with sickness.

He was despised like a shameful person,

and we too regarded him as worthless.

⁴Surely he has carried our illness and endured our torments;

yet we thought he was struck down and afflicted by God.

⁵But in fact he was wounded because of our wrongdoing;

he was crushed because of our evil acts.

The punishment that gave us peace was upon him

and by his bruises we find peace.

⁶We have all gone astray like sheep;

we have all turned to our own way,

and the Lord has laid all our evil on him.

⁷He was oppressed and afflicted,

Yet he did not open his mouth;

like a lamb that is led to the slaughter,

and like a sheep that is silent before its shearers

he did not open his mouth.

⁸By a perversion of justice he was taken away.

Who could have imagined his future?

For he was cut off from the land of the living,

struck down for the transgression of my people.

⁹They made his grave with the wicked

and his tomb with the rich,

even though he had done no violence,

and spoken no lies.

¹⁰Yet it was the will of Yahweh to crush him with pain.

When you make his life an offering for sin,

he shall see his offspring, and shall extend his life;

through him Yahweh's purposes shall prosper.

¹¹Out of his anguish he shall see light;

he shall find satisfaction through his knowledge.

My righteous servant shall make many righteous

and shall bear their iniquities.

¹²Therefore I will apportion him a share of what goes to the great,

and he shall divide the spoil with the strong;

because he poured himself out to death,

and was listed among the transgressors;

yet he bore the sin of many

and prayed for the transgressors. ²¹

From all the songs Isaiah wrote it is not clear who the servant represents—whether it be the corporate people of Israel or a particular person. Either way, Second Isaiah produced a powerful image of the relationship between suffering and redemption that inspired both corporate and personal life. In the cases where Second Isaiah clearly refers to the corporate suffering of Israel, he departs from the predominant tradition of the prophets in that he resists the idea that the suffering of Israel is punishment for her sins.

21. This is my translation.

Yet, if the Servant at times represents the suffering people of Israel, clearly the figure of the Servant in the song above goes beyond simply a symbol for Israel's corporate suffering. Rather the servant functions as a scapegoat in the tradition of Job and Abel and Joseph. It is a classic many-against-one situation of the kind that René Girard analyzed. It is "we," the people, who *mistakenly* believed that the Servant is guilty and that God is punishing him. But the servant is clearly innocent (Isaiah 53:4, 8, 9, 11) and God is in fact the one who vindicates the Servant and exalts him (52:13). As with any scapegoating process the punishment of the people, inflicted on the one, is what unites them and brings peace (53:5b). But the truth is, in persecuting him they have all together, like sheep, gone astray and committed a "perversion of justice" (53:8). It is only because the Lord has given the Servant a future and brought justice[22] out of this injustice that they can see this truth about themselves and about the innocent Servant, their victim.

The puzzling element in this song is that in the end of verse 6 and the beginning of verse 10 we suddenly get the impression that Yahweh has joined sides with the persecutors and their perversion of justice: "The Lord has laid on him the iniquity of us all" and "It was the will of the Lord to crush him with pain." If this were what was meant then we would have a case of God knowingly acting unjustly—participating in a sacrificial and evil killing of an innocent person.[23] A more troubling view of God is hard to imagine.

But the other way of reading it is to see Yahweh as being on the side of the Servant but permitting the persecution because the Servant too is in league with Yahweh to change the whole dynamic here—to make many righteous as a result of his nonviolent stance. His love for his enemies is the vehicle by which (53:10) the "will of the Lord"—not the persecutors—"shall prosper." This collaboration between Yahweh and the suffering Servant is certainly one that goes

---

22. It is helpful to know that the word translated "righteousness" and "righteous" in Hebrew is the same word that is translated "just" and "justice." The Hebrew doesn't distinguish between these concepts.

23. Mark Heim says, "This is a God who has read Nietzsche and agrees." See Heim *Saved from Sacrifice*, 99.

back to the beginning of the Servant's life. "He grew up before him like a young plant" (53:2). And because of his remarkable suffering the kings and nations see something unheard of and completely new (52:15). So the nonviolent servant of Yahweh becomes a servant of the nations, and the wicked—including his persecutors. In bearing the wickedness they inflict upon him his life is poured out as a gift-offering and intercession for them (53:12).

Isaiah thus takes the remarkable step of working out the implications of universal hope already present and implicit in Israel's idea of God as universal creator. The creator of all, in whose image all humanity is created, seeks the redemption of all through the nonviolent suffering of his faithful Servant/servants. As we will see in the next section, this hope is at the center of the God revolution taken up by Jesus of Nazareth.

Discussion Question

What strikes you most about Isaiah's vision of hope? In what ways do you imagine innocent suffering might make a difference to a violent world?

Drawing Some Threads Together

In Isaiah's context the sense that God, the giver of life, is truly beyond the conflicts of history allows the Jewish faithful to turn their attention from the immediate systems of exchange in the pagan world to a posture of hope. The god who can be manipulated is a part of our economic transactions rather than the ground of hope. The god who can be manipulated has a kind of "thingness" like any other thing—an idol. Such a god is inherently in conflict with other things and enclosed in his own "thingness." Such a God can only burn the bush down. What Isaiah suggests to us is that the poured-out life of the Servant of Yahweh might be a witness to the true nature of the greater mystery that ought to be called God (capital G).

But Wait! There's More! ... Further Treasures in the Hebrew Bible

We have reached the end of our brief look at the Old Testament. Before moving on to the section on Jesus it is worth mentioning some of the other treasures to investigate if you have some time on your hands.

The writings of *the prophets* are extensive. Good copy editors were hard to find. We mentioned Isaiah at some length earlier. Within the rest of the writings you will find powerful expressions of the struggle to reform the Hebrew faith. Their two principal— and closely related—concerns are: (1) to challenge any return to paganism in the form of worshipping idols or sacrificing to gods. Such tendencies were often connected to the influence of neighboring empires; and (2) to challenge injustice that oppressed the poor or failed to deal kindly or hospitably with foreigners or visitors or that desecrated creation/the land. The protest movement played a key role in the development of the Jewish faith.

The books of *Joshua, Judges, 1 & 2 Samuel, 1 & 2 Kings* have strung together, in a kind of history, a bunch of juicy and often brutal *hero stories and sagas*. This is the R-rated section of the Bible—at least in parts. However, before you rush off to check it out, it is worth noting that Christian readers down the ages have tended not to treat stories like the mass murder of whole cities, hammering a nail through the head of a sleeping man, and killing one's daughter for a human sacrifice as examples to be followed. Do not try this at home! Christian readers have typically found in these stories hidden, symbolic and sometimes allegorical meanings related to their own lives. The virtues and the ideas about God assumed in some of the stories do not always fit well with either Jesus's own life and theology or with other central moments like the Ten Commandments. The diverse library of Scripture has demanded complex reading strategies from those who take it seriously.

The Old Testament also has its own hymnbook. The *Psalms* are ancient songs or chants that give powerful expression to the struggle to live life before God. You might want to check out Psalms 19, 22, 23, 40, 41, 42, 72, 100, 121, 127, 130, 131, 137, and 139.

The story of *Jonah* is a hilarious parable-like story that broadens the canvas of divine concern beyond Israel and parodies the folly of its principal character. Jonah the foolish "prophet" is a kind of a foil for Yahweh's generosity and mercy.

We have already mentioned another parabolic story—*Job*. This is a powerful exploration—if you can get through all the long speeches—of the problem of evil and suffering in a world created and governed by God. Why do good people suffer?

The *Song of Solomon* is a poetic celebration of erotic love. Along with it are collections entitled *Proverbs* and *Ecclesiastes* associated with the figures of Solomon and Qoholeth (the Teacher). They consist of wise and pithy sayings regarding practicality and prudence in everyday life.

There are also some inspiring stories that explore the challenges created by the exile for those living within the empires of Babylon and Persia. *Daniel* and *Esther*, whose stories are told in books named after them, are heroes of faithfulness and resistance.

Resources

Video: A thirty minute talk on the Christian understanding of the mystery of God and why it matters is available at the link in the footnote.[24]

Book: For a really helpful account of this section of Isaiah and of the Old Testament's treatment of violence you might like to read *Saved from Sacrifice: A Theology of the Cross* by S. Mark Heim.[25]

---

24. Bishop Robert Barron. "The Mystery of God." https://www.youtube.com/watch?v=2BQSqHrU7ns.

25. See especially Heim, *Saved from Sacrifice*, 64–104.

2

The Center of the God Revolution

In which a small group of Galilean peasants become convinced that the creator of the universe had lived a human life among them, suffered directly at the hands of their distorted human existence, been killed by them, and had yet been given back to them so that they might also share in his indestructible life of peace.

or

In which God became human so that humans might become divine and creation fully alive.

Following Jesus

Introduction

THE NEW TESTAMENT PICKS up the story at a time when the hope generated by Isaiah and others is very much alive. Four hundred years have passed since the re-establishment of temple life in Jerusalem again and the last events of the Hebrew Bible. Alexander the Great has conquered most of the world. Greek culture has shaped the known world. Since then Rome has come to power. The temple that was rebuilt after the exile has been magnificently developed by Herod to become an architectural triumph of the ancient world and a powerful but ambiguous symbol of both Jew-ish faith and Roman oppression.

Under the shadow of this temple the Jewish people are pro-foundly unsettled. The hopes of Isaiah remain unrealized and in-complete. Israel is a province of the Roman Empire and controlled with brutal force.

Various responses to the situation are represented by differ-ent groups and revolutionary violence is never far from the sur-face. For Jesus's contemporaries their hope is focussed on a new word—"messiah"—which means anointed one, or simply king. It represents hope for a new and future king in the tradition of David. Hope, for most, is still focussed on restoring the nation's political sovereignty. This political nationalism sits alongside more pious movements associated with the Torah and purity of Jewish identity. Since the major reforms associated with Ezra (428 BC), the purity of religious rituals and faith have become increasingly important. This emphasis is a particular feature of the Pharisee movement.

What Jesus Did

When Jesus turns up in public life he connects with all the main strands of the public life. He acts like a Rabbi (a teacher of the law) and he acts like a Prophet (a critic of the society and its institu-tions). He even connects with their hope for a messiah, although he's very cagey about being called "Messiah." But in all these roles and domains we find him breaking the rules. He is an anarchic (or better subversive) rabbinic prophet of a practically unrecognizable messianism. His approach could be summed up in the sentence: the completion of God's work is arriving among you but not as you expect it. Behind all of his subversive moves we can discern the vision of Second Isaiah and the Servant of Yahweh.

Let's begin by looking at messianic hope. Mark, the writer of the earliest of the four biographical interpretations of Jesus, begins with a powerfully political statement. He announces that what he is writing is an "evangel" (public announcement of good news). This is both a term he knew from Isaiah's messages of hope as well as a Greek term used by the Roman Caesars who were known to call themselves "Son of God." Mark summarizes Jesus's message in a single sentence in Mark 1:15: "The time is fulfilled, and the reign of God has come near; repent and believe in the evangel." Jesus arrived when Israel's hopes for the reign of God, brought about by a messianic figure, were at fever pitch. According to the scholars who counted the years, a jubilee year, or "year of Yahweh's favor" was due. Every seventh year was a Sabbath year and after seven sevens (forty nine or fifty in round figures) Israelites paid particular attention to hopes of restoration and God's reign returning to Jerusalem. In that context Luke—another who offers a biographical interpretation of Jesus's life—tells of Jesus's return to his home town, Nazareth.

Nearly Killed after His First Sermon

Jesus arrives at the Synagogue and is given the scroll of the prophet Isaiah to read. He opens it at chapter 61 and reads:

> The Spirit of the Lord is upon me,
> because he has anointed me
> to bring good news to the poor.
> He has sent me to proclaim release
> to the captives
> and recovery of sight to the blind
> to let the oppressed go free,
> to proclaim the year of the Lord's favor. (Luke 4:18–19)

His sermon on the text amounts to one sentence: "Today this Scripture has been fulfilled in your hearing." We hear that this created quite a buzz (the idea that "they all spoke well of him" is probably a mistranslation). His words are understood as words of grace but that was not necessarily a good thing. The people are puzzled and amazed that he is saying such things.

Why? Why does his hometown seek to kill him after his first sermon? Jesus upsets the hopeful Jews of Nazareth for two closely related reasons.[1] Firstly, he cuts Isaiah short in mid-sentence. He eliminates the end of the sentence in which the prophet continues ". . . and the day of the vengeance of our God." The hope of the poor folk of Galilee is to see God's revenge on their powerful enemies. Jesus does not share this hope. Secondly, he goes on to teach that being a local (as he was) or even belonging to the nation of Israel gives no exclusive right to the "Lord's favor." In other words he strengthens the vision of Isaiah in the direction both of a non-retributive God and in the direction of a universal hope for all peoples. This is not at all a mainstream view on God's reign. For taking this line he is nearly lynched at the beginning of his public ministry.

Stories and Unsettling Metaphors

Jesus's idea of God's reign is strange. So he teaches it in strange stories and metaphors we call parables—stories that puzzle and provoke thought.

Read Luke 10:30–37

When asked to summarize "the Law" the standard Jewish response was something like this from Luke 10:27: "Love the Lord your God with all your heart, and all your soul and all your strength and all your mind, and love your neighbor as yourself." One day Jesus is asked by an expert teacher on the Law: "But who is my neighbor?" (Luke 10:29). To this question too there was a standard answer: your fellow Israelite. But Jesus answers by telling a story. It is famously known as "The Good Samaritan." In the story a man is beaten and left to die on the side of the road. After various Jewish religious leaders pass by, the hero of the story turns out to be not a fellow Israelite but a Samaritan, who, at great cost to himself, aids the man in his distress. Samaritans were the people Jews loved to hate. Jesus does not just say that Samaritans are the neighbors they should love. He is more provocative than that. He tells a story in

1. Hardin, *The Jesus Driven Life*, 59–62.

which the Samaritan—the despised enemy—models true neighbor-love, which is indeed nothing less than enemy-love at great personal cost.

Discussion Question

Can you imagine a contemporary equivalent of this radically subversive story?

Transgression as a Way of Life

For Jesus, God's reign started now. It crossed boundaries of purity. In this world purity was not so much a matter of hygiene as of separating good and evil in the religious/moral life. The reign of God challenged the institutions that were supposed to be central to that hope (i.e., the temple and its worship). Jesus was notorious for befriending those who were excluded from the public life of his people. He is known for befriending a Samaritan woman and many prostitutes. He is known for touching lepers—excluded from society because of their skin disease—and making them clean. Stories are told throughout the Gospels of the work of the creator through him. He is a healer. He is able to control natural forces in a way no other person can. He is known for welcoming and forming friendships with "sinners." Just as contact with Jesus heals the lepers, so contact with Jesus makes a notoriously dishonest tax-man and collaborator—Zacchaeus—into a repentant and generous citizen. Jesus is famous for taking into his own hands the declaration of forgiveness. On behalf of God, whom he called Abba using an intimate (but not necessarily informal) term for father, he forgives people without reference to the normal channels in which God's forgiveness is expressed—the temple rites of atonement. In fact Jesus has little time for the normal channels. As his ministry reaches its climax, he stages a dramatic public protest in the great temple at Jerusalem. The place that, in Jesus's thinking, ought to be a celebration of the gracious life of God for his people and for all people—a house of prayer—has become little more than a market-place in which God is available to the highest bidders.

Discussion Question

Are you surprised that Jesus was crucified?

University on the Road

Like any Rabbi, Jesus gathered disciples about him. Following a Rabbi was the first-century equivalent of a tertiary education. Those who did well at their earlier schooling in the Synagogue were asked to follow a Rabbi. Jesus selected his disciples primarily from among the school dropouts—working the fishing boats in the family business. He wandered the roads of Galilee and Israel while they sought to learn his way and imitate him.

Pacifism at the Dawning of a New Age

The Gospel writers gathered Jesus's teaching together in what has been called the "Sermon on the Mount"—or the "Sermon on the Plain" depending on which Gospel you are reading. In them we see the same radical pacifism that was suggested by Isaiah's Servant. The reign of God, according to Jesus, is accessible to the poor in spirit, the mourners, the meek, those desperate for righteousness, the merciful, the pure in heart, the peacemakers and the persecuted. Like any Rabbi, Jesus had his particular take on the Torah. The persecuted and poor who followed him were called not just to love their neighbors but their enemies and persecutors. In Matthew 5:43–44 he says, "You have heard that it was said, 'You shall love your neighbor and hate your enemy.' But I say to you, love your enemies and pray for those who persecute you."

Here Jesus is not simply repeating the Torah; he is interpreting it and revising it. He is part of an argument about the very nature of God and God's way. The reason he offers for his radical "enemy love" is simply the notion of God as creator and therefore as fundamentally the giver of life for all. The purpose of enemy love is, according to verse 44, "so that you may be children of your Father in heaven; for he makes his sun rise on the evil and on the good, and sends rain on the righteous and the unrighteous." As we saw earlier, that notion of God as creator had profound implications for everyday life. Monotheism does not simply imply a universal hope for all peoples and for all creation in the end (as it did for Isaiah). To Jesus it implied a movement now beyond Israel to her enemies. For Jesus the reign of God was dawning in the present.

For Jesus the Torah and the Prophets were incomplete. Jesus had come to fulfil them (Matthew 5:17) and his account of the kingdom with its radical peace-making and reconciliation lies at the center of a fulfilled Torah.

Jesus's account of God's gracious reign is one that is resistant to the power of money and the anxieties it breeds (Matthew 6:24). Trusting in Abba-God frees one both from anxieties about survival (Matthew 6:25–34) as well as anxieties that would hinder relationships (Matthew 7:1–5). These teachings, he says, provide both a solid foundation—like a house on a rock—and a narrow but life-giving way.

Discussion Question

Given Jesus's expectations of the arrival of God's reign and his convictions regarding loving enemies, how can his followers be anything but pacifists of some kind?

Jesus the Protestor

Jesus's trust in Abba took him to Jerusalem. He could not share the hope of Israel without going there. The Gospels also record his consistent sense that he knew he would be killed. At Jerusalem he did two very significant things (apart from dying):

1. He led a public protest against the injustice and inaccessibility of the temple system and its economy, tipping over the tables of the money changers and chasing out the animals with a stock whip. "Inaccessibility" sounds, to modern ears, like a very abstract word associated with the contemporary discourse of "health and safety." However, exclusion from the temple was a profound issue of justice and righteousness for Jesus.

2. In a less public way he celebrated the Passover meal—a festival to commemorate Israel's origin as slaves liberated from Egypt—with his disciples. However, he reinterpreted the meal to refer not to the Exodus—the symbol of their liberation from slavery and formation as a people—but to himself and his approaching death. Jesus interpreted his own death as the key to a new and transformed people of God. The reign of God would come but not as anyone else expected. Again, it is hard not to see the Servant of Isaiah in the background.

As it happened Jesus was killed, and it was a coordinated effort. The Jewish leaders brought him to the Roman rulers.

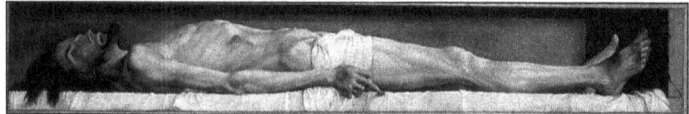

Of course all of these extraordinary ideas would have been lost forever to history if something completely unheard of didn't happen next. I suspect many readers will be thinking "resurrection." We will get to that. However, there is something else to consider first. What the Jewish followers of Jesus did that is so extraordinary that some think it impossible is that, shortly after his death, they began to worship him as God (capital G) while at the same time stressing their loyalty to their Jewish faith in one creator of all.

Worshipping Jesus

Jews Who Worship a Human Being

This requires some explanation. You will recall that the idea of God that Jesus and his followers inherited from Second Isaiah and the exile was more about what God did than a philosophical idea of "godness." For Israel, their God was both the creator of them as a people as well as the creator of everything else. There is only one God for two simple reasons: (1) God creates everything else; and (2) God is supreme over everything else. Where Greeks and other pagan nations might imagine a group of gods with one more powerful than others, Israel in the long run understood Yahweh to be exclusively creator and exclusively supreme over all other things. This Jewish logic created an increasingly clear distinction between God and any other entity—whether it be called a god or an angel or whatever. Yahweh was in a category of his own because of what he did. Although it was impossible to avoid thinking of Yahweh in human terms (anthropomorphically) it was deemed a religious duty—for both theological and moral reasons—to avoid imaging him.

A Complicated God

However, for ancient Israelites humans were neither the only nor the highest creatures in creation. Their view of the cosmos included the existence of angels and patriarchs who had ascended to heaven. They also talked about entities like Yahweh's Wisdom and Word. However, the distinction between the two kinds was strict.[2] Angels and patriarchs were creatures. They did not create the world and any authority they had was subservient to God. However, God's Word and Wisdom, on the other hand, although personified, were seen as *aspects* of God. In short God was singular but not simple. Differentiations could be made within God, but God remained unimaginably unique and singularly sovereign.

The Practice of Worshipping Jesus

In Hebrew thought it was taken for granted that worship was reserved for God alone, yet very early on in the story of the Christian community the followers of Jesus worshipped Jesus as God. They sang hymns to him and prayed to him. By the time the New Testament was written it was accepted that Jesus had divine authority and status—not only sharing in the divine name (YHWH) and participating in divine judgment in the end, but it was also assumed that he participated in the act of creation itself. Internally, holding their Jewish view of God together with their worship of Jesus created a great challenge for Christian thinking. We will say more about this later; however, alongside the internal challenge to their thinking, this worship also created an enormous external challenge.

2. On this, see Bauckham, *Jesus and the God of Israel*, 13–17.

Resource

Jesus and the God of Israel by Richard Bauckham (2008)

On Not Being Very Good Romans

Romans demanded that citizens of their empire tolerate other people's gods within their everyday practices. All gods were welcome. Christian and non-Christian Jews stood against that inasmuch as they refused to participate in the rituals of the various deities. However, to keep peace and because of their peculiar idea about God, the Romans made an exception for Jews, not requiring them to attend the temples of the gods. For a while Christians could piggyback on this exception. The Romans called both Christian and non-Christian Jews "atheists" because of their rejection of the empire's pluralism. In this context pluralism meant getting along with other people's gods; it meant essentially buying into a smorgasbord of multiple deities. Worshipping gods was not like belonging to a religious club. Attending temple rituals for various gods was just one of the things you did to be a good citizen in the cultural world of the Roman Empire. It was not a private distinctive but a common public practice.

What made things worse, and more complicated, for Christians was the kind of human being they worshipped. They believed that the sole creator God had lived a human life as a peasant Galilean who was ultimately crucified. This made him effectively either a slave or a criminal as crucifixion was reserved primarily for the enemies of the empire and for slaves, should their masters want it. From a Roman point of view, the Christian God was a non-person who stood for everything Rome despised.

From a Jewish perspective, this idea of God living a human life was unprecedented. Calling Jesus "Messiah" was one thing. Messiah or king merely referred to a historical figure within Israel's story of hope. Giving Jesus a place in God's own life and rule over the cosmos was another thing altogether. This process turned their minds inside out.

They did not think of God as a "simple soul." God had a complexity they had hitherto not imagined. And at the center of that complexity was the human being, Jesus of Nazareth.

"Something of extraordinary cultural significance occurred when Christianity succeeded in both preserving and overturning the religious logic of theophany, by offering humanity a vision of the face of God, but one visible only in the face of a crucified peasant and thereby in the face of every neighbor." —DAVID BENTLEY HART[3]

Resurrection: The Real Beginning

Why such an extraordinary revolution? It is time to return to that word "resurrection." If there were a logical place to start this whole exploration of Christianity it would be with the experience of resurrection. The resurrection redefined the lives of the first disciples of Jesus, it redefined God, and it redefined how they read their Scriptures. It is not the temporal first point in the story of Christian or Jewish faith (nor is it the first chapter in this book for that matter), but it is the logical first point that gives meaning to all the rest. The experience of the resurrection, however, was multidimensional. It had a density to it that we need to unravel. We will do so under four headings.

Justice

The first thing "resurrection" meant for Jews was final *justice*. They waited for the bodily resurrection of all people when God finally established justice—i.e., made things right. To raise the dead is akin to creation from nothing in the story of Genesis. Death, for Jews, is effectively a fading into nothingness. Jews did not traditionally

3. Hart, "Seeing the God."

believe in eternal souls. God is the only eternal one. Their hope for justice lay in God's action to raise all people to a new bodily life—resurrection. When they met Jesus again after his death they called it resurrection, even though he was the only one raised! Justice was coming but in a way no one expected. Of course Jesus had been saying exactly this all along.

Vindication

The second thing the resurrection experience meant was simply *vindication*. Jesus was right in what he did and said. The God of Israel acted in a way that aligned Yahweh with Jesus of Nazareth. The God of all creation was like Jesus. Jesus was indeed the agent of God's salvation in the world. The flip side of the vindication of Jesus is the judgment of humanity. If the resurrection demonstrates that God is like Jesus, it equally declares that God is unlike his killers. The resurrection is a revelation both of the nature of God and of humanity.

Forgiveness

The third thing the resurrection experience meant was *forgiveness*. You can see this in the way the early Christians talked about it. It was totally and terrifyingly unexpected and undeserved and yet they experienced it as a peaceful gift. This experience of forgiveness came in spite of—or better, alongside and hand in hand with—the experience of judgment. Forgiveness is only forgiveness because there is also judgment. Those who had a few days earlier abandoned Jesus when he gave his life away to his Roman killers were deeply and profoundly lost. They had contributed to the taking of his life. However, the resurrection was not an act of retribution from God. All their previous understanding would lead them to expect God to give them what they deserved. Justice, they might well have thought, meant punishment—i.e., retribution. What they experienced was that God gave Jesus back to them in peace. If retribution means "giving back" in a way that corresponds to what has been given, then the resurrection turns out to be the opposite of retribution. God is unchanged by what they have done to him. Jesus gave his life according to the will of his Father, and now God gives Jesus again. The disciples could only conclude that the resurrection is the answer of God to Jesus's prayer from the cross in Luke 23:34, "Father forgive them, for they know not what they are doing." The first repeated greeting of the risen Jesus (John 20:19, 21) is "Peace be with you." The first preaching of the apostles is repeatedly summarized as a contrast between what they did—crucifying him—and what God did—raising him for their salvation (i.e., wholeness and healing). We might summarize these three aspects of the resurrection experience by saying that the resurrection was the decisive act of divine restorative justice. We are reminded of Jesus's words, in Luke 19:42, as he wept before entering Jerusalem: "They do not know the things that make for peace." It looks as if the death and resurrection of Jesus is God's response to this observation also. Perhaps they are precisely "the things that make for peace."

Defeating Death

The fourth dimension to the experience of the resurrection is the "conquest of death." It is effectively the united meaning of the three previous aspects. The experience of divine justice that comes to them in the form of the gift of Jesus's as forgiveness from beyond the horizon of death is deeply shocking. It means nothing less than the victory of God over the domination that death has over our lives. Although most of us are not consciously afraid of dying, we probably have some sense of the deep anxiety surrounding death that finds diverse cultural expression. According to the writer of the letter to the Hebrews (Hebrews 2:14–15), the fear of death holds us in lifelong slavery. Death, says St. Paul, has a sting, a bondage called "sin." To transform the horizon of death, as God did in raising Jesus, is to effectively de-fang death and liberate us from the bondage that this deep-seated anxiety creates in us.

Death, of course, does not merely shape our personal psychology, but also effects the way we structure our political and economic lives, and—perhaps most obviously—our military lives. So the disempowerment of death announces not merely a new freedom for individuals but a new order in the world. Even while Christians were still dying, especially while Christians were still being martyred, Paul declares death to be defeated (2 Timothy 1:10, 1 Corinthians 15: 54–57). Their willingness to die for Christ was the sign of the death of death. What Robert Jenson says of "the Gospel" could equally well be said of the resurrection. "The Gospel makes peace a possibility by telling us that we *do not have to defend ourselves*, by telling us that our lives are hid with God in Christ."[4]

"The Gospel makes peace a possibility by telling us that we *do not have to defend ourselves*, by telling us that our lives are hid with God in Christ." —ROBERT JENSON

Discussion Questions

How do you see the power/control/anxiety of death present in your own life? Your family? Your society? Global political and economic structures?

Interlude: Watch the Movie *Midnight Special*[5]

The science fiction movie *Midnight Special* (spoiler alert) tells the story of a boy with special powers. It is a powerfully atmospheric movie with a strong sense of the human emotions surrounding the boy and his family. It is never clear what the nature of the boy's powers are. He seems to be able to sense and tune into electronic communications, especially state secrets, and on occasions bright light comes out of his eyes. He has been adopted by a wacky

4. Jenson, *Systematic Theology*, 210.

5. Warner Bros, 2015.

religious cult that interprets his mysterious utterances as signs by which to guide their lives. He is a kind of a saviour-figure for them. However the FBI is chasing him for his ability to hack into their state communications or perhaps for other more sinister reasons. We do not know. In the end the boy realizes that he comes from another world—a world that is overlaid on top of our world. The moment of unveiling—apocalypse—comes with the FBI in hot pursuit of the boy and his family. In that moment the towering structures of the hidden world are revealed for all to see. The boy is taken away and the visibility of the other world is lost again. We are left with the FBI trying to go through their processes, knowing they have seen something they can never forget but are at the same time unable to admit or articulate.

Discussion Questions

What does this experience of the apocalypse of a hidden world mean? How is it like or unlike the experience of the resurrection?

Certainly the apocalyptic experience of the movie does not fit within the world they have known. It expands their horizon in significant ways. It shocks them into a kind of silence. But while analogous, the experience described in the movie *Midnight Special* also differs radically from the resurrection experience. The discovery of an alien world overlaid upon their own one, amounts, in the end, merely to further items in the universe and to hitherto unknown technology. It gives rise to possible new threats to be considered. What it doesn't do—but what the resurrection does do—is introduce them to a new world in which the moral fabric of the universe is different from all they had hitherto imagined. What it doesn't do is draw them with an apparent inevitability towards becoming different people.

The resurrection, on the other hand, is an encounter with that from which the universe gains its meaning. Its impact is to change those who experience it from the inside out. The power of death to threaten and so to define their existence and imprison them in a range of anxieties has been undone for them.

There are several stories of the resurrection in the New Testament and each brings out different aspects of the resurrection experience. However, possibly the most influential and significant story is the only appearance of Jesus to someone who didn't know him before his death. Saul of Tarsus—the first great Christian theologian, later known as Paul—has an experience that is different in some respects, but identical in structure. It is an experience of the risen Christ embracing and transforming Saul, his persecutor. We will discuss the conversion of Paul in the next section when we will expand on his ideas.

So What?

We have reached the central moment of the God revolution. If the resurrection is true then what was glimpsed by Isaiah and by the greatest of the writers of the Old Testament is not merely a theory but an event. It touches history. What our lives depend on is not simply God (indeed God is not simple). What matters is the fact that the creator of the universe is healing our world and addressing our problem of violence by a process of suffering love and nonviolent forgiveness. And, I would posit that if we are to open our lives to it and believe it we will not simply have a new theory but we too will be drawn into it. We will be undergoing this forgiveness of God and slowly learning to love our enemies as God does. When Saul of Tarsus became the spokesperson for this new movement under the name Paul he summarized the situation beautifully in 2 Corinthians 5:19: "God was in Christ [i.e., the Messiah or King] reconciling[6] the world to himself."

Because the resurrection profoundly changed the way the first Christians saw everything, especially the way they saw Jesus, it also shaped the way they told the story of Jesus. The resurrection is not a peripheral addition to the story. In fact, were it not for the experience of resurrection the stories would never have been told. Without the resurrection we would have no Gospels. They are stories written to spell out the nature of the revolution. If God was in Jesus what did that look like? If God is *like Jesus* what does that look like? We see the impact most clearly if we go back for a moment to the stories of his death.

Death through Resurrection Eyes

What we notice when we look back at the climactic stories of Jesus's life is that—like the rest of the stories but more so—the moments leading up to his death are loaded with symbolic meaning and dripping with irony. The true king of the future arrives in Jerusalem on a humble donkey, weeping (Luke 19:42) because his people do not know "the things that make for peace." As he moves through the crowds they cry out (Luke 19:38) "blessed is the one who comes in the name of the Lord."[7] The soldiers who put royal

6. Reconciling here refers to a reorientation that returns the world, first of all but not exclusively the human world, to a positive relationship to the creator and to God's life, where that world has been distorted into, often entrenched, destructive patterns.

7. Those with ears to hear might appreciate that the Psalm which the

colors on him and mock him with a crown of thorns have no idea of the irony of their actions. The inscription on his cross—"King of the Jews"—is meant to be sarcastic but it tells the truth. Caiaphas the religious leader offers the verdict of *realpolitik* (John 11:50), "it is better that one man should die for the people."

Such scapegoating is simply common sense for a religious politician. And yet, the ironic truth is that, as Isaiah knew, the suffering and death of one was in fact what would redeem the people. It would create of them a true people of God infinitely more stable than a society built on violence. John's Gospel seems most aware of the symbolism of the temple priest. From it we read that Jesus has a "seamless robe"—i.e., a priest's robe—and that like the atonement lamb he remained flawless without a broken bone. Moreover, in John's Gospel he dies on a Thursday at the time the lamb is sacrificed in the temple.

---

crowd is citing (Psalm 118:36) refers to the priest who comes out of the temple with YHWH on his forehead.

Finally, in a symbolic moment, when Jesus gives his life to his Abba/Father in death, the curtain of the temple is torn from top to bottom. The separation between worship—represented by the ritual of the temple—and history has gone. Jesus has chosen to die as a kind of priestly sacrifice of thanksgiving but he does so by taking the priestly realm into the historical and political world. In place of a veil of secrecy, we are told, we too get to participate in this life of God with us. The life of the world gets to encounter something it might not otherwise have seen.

In short, when the stories of Jesus get written down, they are told in ways that see signs of the deeper truth of the resurrection everywhere. Jesus is the true king unrecognized. Jesus is the priest doing God's work of restoration and healing. What is historically a tragedy is—from the "God perspective"—the beginning of a new creation, like that dramatized in the ancient temple and hoped for by the prophets.

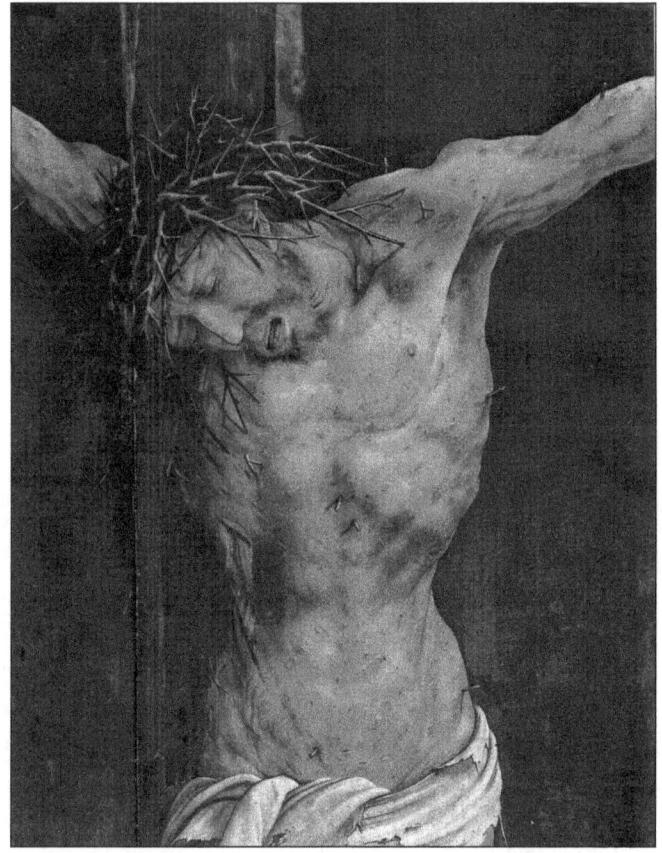

What's love got to do with the Easter story? Here's a five-minute reflection from Dr. Ben Myers.[8]

Raised in a Garden

If the crucifixion story is dripping with irony, the story of the resurrection is full of symbolism. Jesus rises in a garden and is mistaken for a gardener.

8. Common Grace, "Love Thy Neighbour: Hopeless Love." https://www.youtube.com/watch?v=IJWUTaCJiVc&feature=youtu.be.

In fact, it is the beginning of a new creation. The Garden of Eden story from Genesis is being rewritten. When he greets and commissions the disciples to be people of forgiveness he breathes on them and it is the breath of the Spirit—the same Spirit who hovers over the deep in the creation story (Genesis 1:2). When they eat food together with him their eyes are opened and they start to understand both their Scriptures and his death with new eyes. This contrasts with the story in Genesis 3 where sharing food leads to shame and deception.

Summary

In summary, the turning point around which this venture of faith revolves lies in the experience of God presenting to the first Christians (and perhaps to us also) a life lived from a source outside of our violently structured world, and doing so in a way that opens up a new and different kind of world. The beautiful story is one in which Jesus of Nazareth not only understood something about God (Abba) that others were blind to, he also lived his life in a startling self-abandonment of love. His was the politically unsettling love of costly commitment to those despised people on the underbelly of the world. When it all "hit the fan" in a classic moment of sacrificial violence, he was brutally tortured and executed naked and in public shame.

Where it is potentially comic rather than tragic is the fact that those first disciples, with the egg of this violent world still on their faces, found themselves addressed again by the same Jesus and welcomed into a new world in the midst of the old one. It became for them not the end of it all but the beginning of something new. The next chapter will explore the character of the new thing that was born.

3

The Outcome of the God Revolution

In which the small group of Jesus-followers begin the experiment of living the Jesus-life together, often failing but, at their best, fearless in their friendships, fearless in sharing their possessions, and fearless in their intellectual courage to re-imagine God and the human project.

or

In which the Spirit of God begins to re-program the small group of Jesus-followers with the life of the age to come.

Empowered by the Spirit of God

To Recap

WE HAVE EXPLORED WHAT it means to live one's life in a way that goes beyond mere survival. We then began to explore the notion that we might be dependent on God not merely for our existence but for meaning, purpose, and hope. In order to do this we have taken a more or less historical tour of certain changes in the idea of God in the Jewish tradition. Now, at the center of the God revolution, we have looked at this tradition in the light of the extraordinary claim that God, the sole creator of the universe, lived a human life. Not merely for the fun of it, of course, but for the healing of it. Humanity is so deeply messed up that God's human existence plunges God into profound suffering. On the other side of that suffering, death may be defeated, but not many people know it. The re-creation of humanity is inaugurated but not complete. Humanity needs to be "rebooted" to share again in the peaceful existence it was created for. Somehow Jesus's life must become our life also.

But how does it happen to us?

Dovetailed onto the experience of the resurrection, as the New Testament tells it, is the experience of the Holy Spirit. If the resurrection is an objective event in the sense that it happened to Jesus, first of all and quite regardless of what its impact is on us, then the experience of the Spirit is a subjective experience. By this we don't mean that it is the product of our imagination. But rather that, although it is an experience of God, it happens to our own life and action first of all. It is the work of God "within" us. The Spirit re-works the life of Jesus in us and shapes us to be part of his life and to reflect it in our own way.

The notion that God worked in the world as Spirit was not a new one. The Hebrews already talked of the breath of God in creation and in the prophets. The Hebrew word for breath is *ruach*, often translated Spirit. It was part of the way they understood the complexity of the one God, whose Word and Wisdom and Spirit were all part of God's interaction with creation.

The Spirit of God Is the Spirit of Jesus

Now that the decisive work of God was understood to be the work of God in Jesus of Nazareth they associated the Spirit of God closely with the impact of the risen Jesus upon them. The Spirit that was in *him*, was the same Spirit given to *them*.

The Spirit was given to them as much by Jesus as by God. In a famous resurrection story (John 20:19–23) Jesus is said to breathe the Spirit of God upon them while commissioning them to be practitioners of divine forgiveness.

The Spirit of Jesus Is the Spirit of Reconciliation

Read Acts 2:1–13

The most famous story of the experience of the Spirit is Pentecost. When the disciples were gathered together for this Jewish festival they experienced the Spirit of God giving them miraculous powers to communicate across language barriers, or rather to understand what people are saying in other languages. Although this is not a common experience in the history of Christianity, it is often regarded as representative of the power of Christ to cross cultural barriers and bring about reconciliation between divided groups.

Living out of Control

Another obvious characteristic of the experience of the Spirit was a loss of control. Those filled with the Spirit of God were, like the prophets of old, assumed to be drunk. This makes a lot of sense. If a whole new way of life is breaking into a world shaped in fear under the domination of death, those who have learned to live in the old world cannot simply remain in control and make it happen. It must first of all happen to them. They must abandon control of their lives and entrust their future to the work of the Spirit of Jesus. If the resurrection is true and if the "world-as-it-is" is what crucified Jesus, then those who are beginning to participate in the new world "as it will be" need to be interrupted by God, even "possessed" by God's newness.

Discussion Question

Clearly being out of control (as the word "possessed" provocatively suggests) feels dangerous, and might in certain contexts be so. What does this mean for those considering the venture of Christian faith?

Prayer as Openness

Prayer is the practice of allowing God to interrupt our lives. The agent of that interruption who re-shapes our lives and identities after the likeness of Jesus is the Holy Spirit. In this sense the Spirit of God is the one who liberates us from the past—the past that would otherwise live on in us—to follow Jesus. As one writer (Karl Barth) is reputed to have said, "to fold your hands in prayer" is to be drawn into "an uprising against the world."

Discussion Questions

What kinds of experiences of Christian prayer have you had? Did you understand what was intended by the practice at the time?

The Spirit Inspires Fearlessness and Martyr-Witness

A further distinctive of the experience of the Spirit of God in the stories of the New Testament is a loss of fear (Acts 4:31). If the power of death to dominate us by fear is indeed defeated by the resurrection of Jesus it is to be expected that those filled by the Spirit of Jesus would show signs of fearlessness in the face of violence and death—the same fearlessness that Jesus showed when he "took up his cross" in the face of a social order in which he did not belong. Indeed the New Testament book, *The Acts of the Apostles*, is full of stories of how the disciples could not be silenced by religious and political authorities and sometimes were killed for their efforts. The early church treasured the stories of its witnesses—martyrs—who were faithful to the non-retaliatory life of Jesus even unto death (Acts 7:54—8:1).

Discussion Question

What are the differences between martyrs who die performing acts of terror and the Christian martyrs of the first few centuries?

Paul: Theologian of the Spirit's New Creation

The most famous story of martyrdom in the New Testament is the stoning of the fiery Stephen in Acts 7. There we are introduced to Saul, a young student of the rabbi (teacher) Gamaliel. Gamaliel was famous as an advocate of tolerance. Saul later changes his name to Paul. With the martyrdom of Stephen, some scholars suspect, we glimpse a shift in loyalties and alliances that may have provoked Saul to distance himself from the "Gamaliel School." In the Acts account the next we know of Saul is that he is leading what amounts to a terror snatch-squad. But according to Acts 9:5 he is stopped in his tracks by a light that blinds his eyes and a voice that announces "I am Jesus whom, you are persecuting." This "divine truth" launches him into a new vocation within the community of Jesus-followers. Saul's experience of judgment and forgiveness produces in him the most dramatic interpretation of Jesus.

Paul went on to become the leader of Christian mission to non-Jewish people. His writings were the earliest documents in the New Testament. People like Paul were thinking and writing about Jesus well before the Gospels were written. All the themes we have been observing in the density of the resurrection experience get a thorough development in the letters that Paul wrote to Christian communities.

Everything Is New

For Paul everything is new—creation, human nature, and the people of God! His transition from terrorist to missionary of peace leaves him convinced that the world is being created anew. He writes to the Galatian Christians in Galatians 2:19–20: "I have been crucified with Christ; and it is no longer I who live, but it is Christ who lives in me. And the life I now live in the flesh I live by faith in the Son of God, who loved me and gave himself for me." The contrast between Jesus and the world that crucified him is a contrast Paul takes personally upon himself. He sees himself as crucified with Jesus to become a new person and be adopted into a new world.

Read Romans 5:12–17 and 1 Corinthians 15:22–45

One of the main ways Paul talks about this new beginning is to talk about Jesus as the "second Adam." In Genesis, Adam represents the human project to date and thus the way in which human life is distorted and sinful. We are all living in the wake of Adam and caught up in something problematic. Jesus on the other hand is the *first* to live a truly human life—one of complete trust in the creator and thus of risky love for his fellow human beings. In this sense Jesus inaugurates a new wave of divine creation. Through him God is creating a new human species and a new world. Jesus is another kind of Adam. The world, according to Ephesians 1:10, is being gathered up in Jesus into something new.

Reconciling the World to God

Read 2 Corinthians 5:16–21

The central impulse for this new creation is God's love for the whole cosmos. This Paul understands not as a distant affection but as an active process of forgiveness and reconciliation through the crucifixion and resurrection of Jesus. The cosmos is being reconciled to God. The God who forgave Paul and the crucifiers of Jesus has open arms to embrace all people. No one can now be seen from a "human point of view" but only through the eyes of Jesus Christ. Paul thus sees that all who now share in this new world are caught up in its movement. It is an experience that changes their lives. As people whose boundaries have been made permeable by his life—as people who now exist "in Christ"—they have become "ambassadors" of this work of reconciliation. In all of this, God is creating, out of violent and trapped humanity, concrete expressions of divine justice on earth.

So from now on we don't look at anyone from a human point of view. Even though we once knew Christ from a human point of view, we no longer know him that way. So if anyone is in Christ, there is the new creation: everything old has passed away; see everything has become new! All this is from God who reconciled us to himself through Christ; that is, in Christ God was reconciling the world to himself, not counting their sins against them, and entrusting the message of reconciliation to us. So we are ambassadors for Christ, since God is making his appeal through us; we entreat you on behalf of Christ, be reconciled to God. It was for our sake that God made him to be treated as a sinner, even though he wasn't one, so that in him we might become the justice of God.

—2 Corinthians 5:16–21

The Welcome That Dissolves Barriers and Rivalry

Read Ephesians 2:11–22

The implications of this for Paul and his friends are profoundly social and political. In this newly emerging world the barrier that divided Jews and Gentiles has gone. The rivalry that produced the hostilities has been dissolved by the word of peace spoken from the cross and again by the risen Christ. The fact that in Jesus's death God had entered the worst of human violence as its victim and scapegoat and responded to it with a word of peace, created for them all a whole new freedom before God and one another. God had embraced them in a way that empowered them to embrace one another.

New Equality, New Community

Read 1 Corinthians 12:12–27

The impact of this new situation found its first expression in the life of local communities. Old distinctions that gave status and order to the world were regarded as ultimately irrelevant. Paul summarizes the situation famously in Galatians 3:27: "There is no longer Jew nor Greek, there is no longer slave nor free, there is no longer male and female, for all of you are one in Christ Jesus." The full implications of this revolution took some time to work themselves out. Take, for example, the issue of slavery. It continued in the Roman Empire and the earliest Christians coexisted with the realities of slavery. However, the New Testament offers glimpses of changing relationships between slaves and their masters as they began to see themselves and "brothers and sisters" of a new world. Unequal status for men and women continued, although there are clear signs of this changing in certain respects. Perhaps the most we can say is that as Paul worked out the implications of the God revolution he lit a fuse which still continues to change the world today.

For Paul the reconciliation of Jesus creates a new social phenomenon. It is not like a society or club or business where many people are merely working together for a common cause. He sees it more like an organism in which, as Rowan Williams describes it, no part is "safe" from the rest. We need each other, impact each other, and are gratefully dependent on each other. For this Paul coined the phrase "body of Christ." This was a new space where God could be seen in the world—a temple of a human kind.

Discussion Question

Where in the contemporary world do you see this idea of interconnected and organic community expressed and where do you see the opposite?

Freedom

All this is possible because the power that the Spirit of Jesus gives is the power to be free. "For freedom Christ has set us free," says Paul in Galatians 5:1. This is not freedom to do what I want with my life, but freedom from the struggles of a violent world in order to live in a new world order—to love my neighbor and even my enemy. For Paul it is a liberation for the purposes of self-forgetting. By this is meant not an attack on the self or a loss of self, but rather a turn towards the other and the greater reality in which the self flourishes. It is freedom to be like Jesus and willingly take the subservient and weakest place (see Philippians 2:5–8). This is a complete inversion of Paul's cultural values as a Roman citizen. Paul summarizes this point most memorably in Galatians 5:1: "Christ has set us free to live a free life. So take your stand! Never again let anyone put a harness of slavery on you."[1]

1. From *The Message* translation of the Bible.

A New Economy

For Paul and other New Testament writers the coming of Christ calls for a new economy. This is not, nor should it ever really be, merely a theory. Rather Paul sees this new life as working itself out in new ways of living together. The new ethic and economy is embodied in particular communities. We glimpse this in various places in the New Testament. It is perhaps most famously in Acts—written by a man called Luke. Luke's story probably offers an idealistic summary of the first church. But idealistic or not, the aspirations in the story are an unavoidable implication of the meaning of the resurrection and the experience of the Spirit. In Acts 2:44–47 we read:

> All who believed were together and had all things in common; they would sell their possessions and goods and distribute the proceeds to all, as any had need. Day by day as they spent much time together in the temple, they broke bread at home and ate their food with glad and generous hearts, praising God and having the good will of all the people. And day by day the Lord added to their number those who were being saved.

This is further elaborated in Acts 4:32–35:

> Now the whole group of those who believed were of one heart and soul, and no one claimed private ownership of any possessions, but everything they owned was held in common. With great power the apostles gave their testimony to the resurrection of the Lord Jesus, and great grace as upon them all. There was not a needy person among them, for as many as owned lands or houses sold them and brought the proceeds of what was sold. They laid it at the apostles' feet and it was distributed to each as any had need.

Resource:

Coming Back to Earth: Essays on Church, Climate Change, Cities, Agriculture and Eating by Jonathan Cornford

---

These are stories that flesh out the community-creating power of "the supreme peacemaking gift."[2] They tell of a community that isn't really about abandoning Israel and the project that Israel was. Rather, this new form of community continues to seek to fulfil the purpose of Israel in the first place—to live out the justice of God for the sake of the entire world. Reading these stories in the twenty-first century it is impossible not to be struck by how different this account of life is from the world as we know it. For us privacy of both existence and property is a prized possession. While much could be said about this, I will limit myself to three comments:

(i) Holiness—the different difference: It is important to remember that Israel has always prided itself in being different from the surrounding cultural world. The word for this difference was "holiness," which doesn't so much mean good behavior as different behavior. The first Christians embraced this term but redefined it, taking it in different ways—a different difference if you like—that reflected the difference of Jesus.

(ii) Communism of the Spirit: It is worth noting that this story in Acts is not an account of communism.[3] It goes deeper than that. It is not that people have to abandon their private property as a condition of entry into the community or that this arrangement is maintained by threat of force. It is a product of the freedom they experience "in Christ" and the new mindset it creates. In the words of Acts 4 "no one *claimed* private ownership."

(iii) Justice for the poor: Like Jesus in his relationships with the poor, the community that seeks to embody the justice and

---

2. Williams, *Meeting God in Paul*, 50.
3. Cornford, *Coming Back to Earth*, 18.

reign of God pays special attention to the welfare of its weakest and most vulnerable members—"to each as any had need."

Discussion Questions

Why does this new economy bear so little resemblance to the practices and life of the Christian community today?

Are there notable exceptions now? Or in the past?

As our contemporary economic systems start to destroy us and our planet, do you think there are resources here for wider society? How might they scale up?

Care for the Non-human Creation

From the stories of Genesis 1 to the vision of a new earth in the book of Revelation, it is clear that all of the created world is God's delight and God's project. Our human fear and selfishness is not only destructive of the human community but undermines our pivotal role in the ecology of creation. The twenty-first century has forced Christians to rediscover what has often gone unnoticed especially in the modern world—the call to love not just our human neighbors but our non-human neighbors as well. It is for this also that the Spirit liberates us.

> The recent papal document by Pope Francis, *Laudato si'*, is a powerful expression of a Christian understanding of our relation to the non-human creation in the face of environmental crisis.

The Practices of the Community of the Spirit

Eucharist: Resurrection Re-enacted

This new start is sometimes called a "new covenant"—i.e., coming together—from which we get the term "New Testament." Because the new covenant established in the dying and resurrection of Jesus is the defining fact of the new community they constantly went back to this event. Their practice of doing this was significantly formed by the memory of Jesus celebrating a Passover meal with his disciples prior to his death, and of how he used it as an illustration of his calling to die. Holding the bread he announces that it was his body given for them. The wine he called his blood poured out for them. These things, this life given to death and raised for them, make up the substance of forgiveness and the reality that sustains this "body" that is also called "church."

So when the communities of early Christians met together to eat together, especially when they were no longer welcome in the Jewish synagogues, they would also ritually re-enact that meal of Jesus with his first disciples. In so doing they looked to his promise to be with them and made a clear statement about the event that they understood to be their salvation. In these events they experienced the presence of God's forgiveness in the risen Christ. This mysterious presence of God's salvation they eventually called "sacrament" from the Latin word *sacramentum* meaning mystery.

Baptism—Dying to Live

Just as Paul described his new life as a baptism into Christ and a crucifixion with Christ so that he could rise to share in the new world by the power of the Spirit, so the Christians marked the start of the Christian life with baptism in water. In this they took up and reinterpreted a Jewish ritual. Similarly to the Eucharist, they called this moment of entry into the life of Jesus a sacrament. In the early church they would spend time with new believers for some months, even a year, to encourage and form them in this new way of living, and at the end of this formational period they would often baptize these new Christians on the eve of Easter Sunday, naked before the congregation. Facing the dark night these new followers would renounce the devil and the sinful world of violence and then as they arose from the waters symbolizing death they would be clothed in new robes. These new clothes symbolize "putting on Christ" and his new life. The resurrection defined everything for Christians, so as they became alienated from the rest of Judaism they began to worship together on the first day of the week—Sunday, rather than the Sabbath, Saturday—as it was the day of Jesus's resurrection.

Trinity: The God Revolution Goes Theoretical

> *You think because you understand "one" you must also understand "two," because one and one make two. But you must also understand "and."*—ANCIENT SUFI TEACHING

We have called our study the God revolution. We have looked at the idea of God (with a capital G) in a world that knew only of gods (small g). We have looked at the possibility of peaceful existence in a world shaped by the struggle to survive and a human tendency towards violence. We noted that God although singular need not be conceived, and indeed wasn't conceived, as a simple "individual." There was a lot going on in God. We also noted that Hebrew thinkers were not primarily concerned with the nature of God—what God is—but were more concerned with identifying God by God's action—who God is. However, it was inevitable that the question of God's nature would arise. It did for the Jews, and it certainly did for Christians.

The possibility that God, creator of all, might in some sense be a creature also and live the life of a creature was a thought that pushed to the breaking point the idea of complexity within God's singular life. However, that new thought was not easily dismissed. As we have noted, the Christian experience of the new event in God—Jesus's resurrection—was one that impacted and changed them personally. They understood themselves to be now participating in God's own life. To abandon the original thought would be to abandon their experience of new life and hope. It would mean abandoning the established practice of worshipping the man Jesus as God.

Judaism and Jesus Meet Greek Philosophy

As Christianity spread quickly throughout the Graeco-Roman world, this Jewish mystery created an intellectual challenge for Greeks and Romans also. For Greek-thinking people to understand the Christian faith meant for them to ask about the *nature*—or essence or being—of God. How could they make sense of the facts of both diversity and unity in God? It got more complicated because two languages were involved in the debate—Greek and Latin. The Greek way was to talk of God having one being (*ousia*) and three substances (*hypostases*). The substances were of, course, the Son (incarnate as Jesus of Nazareth), the Spirit (of God and of Christ), and the Father (Jesus's Abba and source of both Son and Spirit and with them creator of all). In Latin, on the other hand, they talked of the three as persons (*personae*) and the oneness of God as substance (*substantia*).

Agreeing on the vocabulary was a first step. However, these terms had connotations that made the whole enterprise really tricky. The really big issue had to do with the meaning of the terms. If the words for the "threeness" in God were a Greek word meaning *substance* and a Latin word meaning *person*, does that mean that God is the jumble of three individuals like marbles in a bag? And if this is so have we lost the singular creator of Jewish faith and replaced it with three gods? On the other hand if the Latin word for persons simply means a "mask," does that mean that there is no significant difference between Father, Son, and Spirit? Are they just temporary masks put on by the one unknown God? What was at stake then was the conviction that God was truly known in Jesus's life and that God was active in this and in their experience of the Spirit among them.

So What Is Real? What Is a Person?

A thinker called Athanasius suggested that persons are not individuals—single separate things like billiard balls on a table. Rather they are what they are only as a product of their relations to others. Relations make them real. The unique identity of each of the divine "persons" lies in their relation to the other "persons" while all share in the common divine life (*ousia*).

This may not seem earth-shattering at first glance. However, hidden away in what might appear to be a cute philosophical puzzle is a second revolution in thinking about both God and humanity. The challenge to think about God after Jesus Christ had now led Christians to think differently about not only God but also about human beings and about reality in general. A new kind of philosophy was born that overturned some of the deep ideas of the Greek world. As we have said, in the Greek imagination a person was not really real, but was a fleeting "mask"—*persona*—an addition to what was really real or substantial. To suggest that God was personal by being essentially "made" of the relations within God means that personal relations are the stuff of reality. In Greek thinking nature had a necessity about it in which freedom did not sit well. Hence, for example, in Greek tragic drama we see a real struggle with the idea that we might be free. Christian thought challenged this by putting the freedom of divine and personal relations at the center of reality. The freedom at the center, however, is not the modern idea of unconstrained freedom to do our own thing but rather the freedom to love and serve the Other.

For all its profound impact on Christian thought, this relational revolution has had a rocky road in the history of thought and philosophy since early Christianity. We need only think of the widespread influence of René Descartes's idea of the self as thinking "substance" to appreciate this. However, exploring these developments is well beyond our task here.

God Is Love: A Non-sentimental Conclusion

It looks as if we have ended with a new philosophy. Has the quest to live a meaningful existence been left behind? Not at all! The theoretical work flows from a simple and practical need to offer an account of the experience of God who is love. It is important for Christians not to be silenced by what others think are the fixed boundaries of the world—and in turn what is possible in it. In short the Christian experience and story must be told in new ways in new contexts. The theory of God as Trinity is the result of telling the story in a Greek context. Such telling is motivated by the conviction that we are given our existence by God as an act of God—i.e., as an act of love. And the existence we are given is a life in which we participate in this love of God and are set free to live and love. We live and become truly human in the love of the Trinity.

The End: So What Can We Hope For?

> *The hope and the doom of the love of friends*
> *Is eating up the marrow of our bones.*—JAMES K. BAXTER[4]

At the end of the Old Testament we saw the development of a great hope. This hope was linked to trust in a God who created *all things* and cared for creation deeply; deeply enough, to redeem through suffering. For Isaiah, that hope went beyond Israel to the nations of the earth.

In the New Testament we see that hope enter into the world of history in the person of Jesus. The two symbols of Israel's hope—messiah and resurrection—are now events in history. In the Christian story God's freedom from the violent world is matched by God's intimate involvement in the world's healing. The God who is free *from* the world is also the God who is free to be *for* the world. God has taken redemption into God's own hands and lived in the world as a suffering servant who confronts and unveils a fallen and violent world. In his life we are already judged and found lacking.

---

4. Baxter, "Song to the Lord God," 572–73.

Differences between Christianity and Judaism

The new community of followers of Jesus that emerges after the resurrection has both continuities and discontinuities with the project of Israel. For all the sad history of conflict between Jews and Christians, Rabbinic Judaism and Christianity are in fact siblings and alternative ways of continuing the story of life with God. However, the differences cannot be minimized. Firstly, we noted in our discussion of the Trinity that the Christian community ended up rethinking the complex nature of the one God. This meant that for them the relations that made God to be God—the love between Father, Son and Spirit—meant that in a strong sense Christians were led to conclude not merely that God loved them but that, as 1 John 4:7-9 puts it, "God is love."

Secondly, Christians developed a different sense of their location in time. Hope took on a new texture. They found themselves living in an interim moment. It is the beginning of the end already. For those who do believe that the messianic hopes of Israel are fulfilled in Jesus, the resurrection is the in-breaking of hope. The content of our hope for the future is present, albeit in an incomplete way, now.

Finally, the nature of what Christians hope for is now irreversibly defined by their experience of the character of God lived out in Jesus of Nazareth. Judged by his life now, they expect to be judged by it in the end. Forgiven by it now, they expect to be redeemed by it in the end.

Personal and Cosmic Hope

If we are to take the resurrection seriously in our own lives the question of what we can hope for becomes more than a curiosity. It is immediately relevant to our present existence and our capacity to act in difficult times. However, it is relevant to our personal existence because it is first of all relevant to a much bigger story of God and creation. Christianity is not about "going to heaven." To be part of the God Revolution is not primarily a question of our own personal survival or flourishing, and certainly not in isolation, but of the flourishing of the world we are part of—God's creation project. These two things are bound up together. We are who we are as "relational beings" inseparable from our social and our biological communities.

Hope in the Jaws of Despair

At this point the contrast between faith and despair becomes stark. Whatever we might say about the influx of divine justice with the resurrection of Jesus, we must conclude that this redemptive process is launched but not completed. Injustice is everywhere. Violence fills the earth. Economic inequality has never been greater. Ecological devastation is threatening to undermine the processes of sustainability that provide structure to the dance of creation. Hope feels harder than ever. Is it darkness before the dawn or will the ubiquitous dystopian novelists from George Orwell to Cormack McCarthy have the last word?

What the resurrection means for both our personal existence and the whole biological and ecological system in which we live and move, is that death itself will not have the last word—now or at our deaths. God who is beyond creation as its source is invested in ensuring the peace of creation both now and at the end. Will God succeed? Will all things be healed and given their true harmony or must we be satisfied with a partial healing and a tragic fate for God's creation?

Universalism?

Arguably the whole direction of the biblical story pushes in the direction of the greater hope—the salvation of everyone and of all things. However, strangely enough the majority view within the history of Christianity has not embraced this conclusion, even though many of the New Testament writers seem to accept—at least in places—that all will be redeemed (e.g., John the Evangelist, John of

Patmos, Paul, and Luke). Paul in particular seems to interpret the experience of the resurrection in this way. However there are some parts of the New Testament that appear to deny this. In particular many argue that because Jesus appears to assume a doctrine of hell we cannot believe in the salvation of all things.

This is both a controversial and a complex issue for the Christian faith. However, because it is so important I want to finish this book with some brief and (admittedly) inadequate comments. I will follow this up with a series of texts that will, I hope, open the reader to, at least the plausibility of, a bigger hope. First the comments:

1. Universalism—the idea that all creation will be redeemed—is not a fringe view. Although it is a minority view it has been held by important and leading Church Fathers from the first few centuries of the church as well as by a stream of thinkers since then. It is more commonly accepted in the Eastern Church than in the West.

2. When Jesus teaches about the arrival of God's reign by means of his ministry he assumes an "age to come." He speaks both of the present and of the future. The adjective to describe the age to come (*aionios* in Greek) can and usually does refer to the *quality* of that age rather than its endless duration. For example when Jesus talks of "eternal life" (*zoe aionios*) we can translate it—the life of the age to come. The translation "eternal" is thus often inappropriate. Thus when Jesus in his *Parable of the Sheep and the Goats,* in Matthew 25:31–46, talks of the destiny of those who mistreated the poor—the goats—a better translation is "the chastisement of the age to come" rather than "eternal punishment." If this is a legitimate translation and chastisement is a temporary process aimed at restoration and correction, then this is not what is often thought of as hell—i.e., unending conscious torment by God.

3. Most Christians thinkers who have believed in universalism do not think of it as a simple pardon or exemption from "hell" but rather think of redemption as a process of transformation

that extends beyond the limit of death but will certainly be finite in duration. It is penultimate, however we imagine it, rather than ultimate. What matters both now and in the age to come is transformation rather than pardon. Pardon merely perpetuates the problems of this age in the age to come.

4. Biblical writers use metaphors of fire and burning to indicate purification and transformation. A common example is the word translated hell (*gehenna*), which is the name for the place where rubbish was burned in the valley near Jerusalem. It should not be assumed that reference to fire is about punishment or destruction. Indeed this purging and transformative idea is made explicit in some places.

The New Testament and Universal Salvation

What follows is simply a collection of examples of places where the New Testament appears to assume and sometimes explicitly express a universal hope. They are worthy of further reflection.

Luke, the Gospel writer, picks up the universal direction of Isaiah's hope when he records John the Baptist declaring, in Luke 3:6, that "*all flesh* shall see the salvation of God." He similarly records, in Acts 3:20–21, Peter preaching about "Jesus, who must remain in Heaven until the time of universal restoration."

Similarly the writer of John's Gospel, in these and other examples looks to a cosmic salvation rather than focussing on the individual. We see it in his use of phrases like "the world" and "all things."

> Here is the Lamb of God who takes away the sin of *the world*. (John 1:29)

> For God so loved *the world* that he gave his only Son, that whoever believes in him may not perish but have eternal life. Indeed, God did not send the Son into the world to condemn *the world*, but in order that *the world* might be saved through him. (John 3:16–17)

The Father loves the Son, and has placed *all things* in his hands. (John 3:35)

I am the light of *the world.* (John 8:12)

And I, when I am lifted up from the earth, will draw *all people* to myself. (John 12:32)

Jesus, knowing that the Father had given *all things* into his hands . . . (John 13:3)

Everything that the Father gives me will come to me, and anyone who comes to me I will never drive away . . . And this is the will of him who sent me, I should lose *nothing of all* that he has given me, but raise it up at the last day. (John 6:37, 39)

For you given him authority over all people to give eternal life to all whom you have given him. (John 17:2)

As we indicated earlier Paul was the one who thought these matters through most thoroughly. One way he does this is to see in the life of Jesus the reversal of the universal sin "in Adam." Thus he hopes for and believes in a new creation of humanity as a whole.

For as *all* die in Adam, so *all* will be made alive in Christ. (1 Corinthians 15:22)

Therefore just as one man's trespass led to condemnation for *all,* so one man's act of righteousness leads to justification and life for *all.* (Romans 5:18)

For God has imprisoned all in disobedience so he may be merciful to *all.* (Romans 11:32)

Finally, Paul could hardly be more explicit about his conviction than when he writes:

Then comes the end, when he hands over the kingdom to God the Father, after he has destroyed every ruler and every authority and power. For he must reign until he has put *all* his enemies under his feet. The last enemy to be destroyed is death. For "God has put *all things in subjection* under his feet." But when it says "*all things* are put in subjection," it is plain that this does not include the one who put *all things* under him. And when *all things* are subjected to him, then the Son himself will also be subjected to the one who put all things in subjection under him, so that God may be *all in all*. (1 Corinthians 15:24–28)

The parallels in Paul's thinking are important. He sets the spread of sin throughout the whole of the human race in parallel to the spread of new life in Christ to all. A partial salvation makes no sense of Paul's hope.

When writing to the Christians in Philippi he takes this universal hope for granted

> . . . so that at the name of Jesus *every* knee should bend, in heaven and on earth and under the earth, and *every* tongue should confess that Jesus Christ is Lord, to the glory of God the Father. (Philippians 2:10)

> He will transform the body of our humiliation that it may be conformed to the body of his glory [or more simply, "his glorious body"], by the power that also enables him to make *all things* subject to himself. (Philippians 3:21)

In the Letter to Timothy it becomes very clear that Paul is not simply talking about hope for those who believe although they have an advance engagement with this hope.

> For to this end we toil and struggle, because we have our hope set on the living God, who is the Savior of *all people*, *especially* of those who believe. (1 Timothy 4:10)

In a similar manner to the tradition of Paul, we read in 1 John an explicit denial of the idea that redemption is limited to the believers

> And he is the atoning sacrifice for our sins, and not for ours only, but also for the sins of the *whole world*. (1 John 2:2)

Similarly, in the Letter to the Hebrews and in Second Peter, hope is clearly universal.

... but in these last days he has spoken to us by his Son, whom he appointed heir of all things, through whom he created the world. (Hebrews 1:2)

The Lord ... is not wanting any to perish but all to come to repentance. (2 Peter 3:9–10)

Finally, it is worth commenting briefly on the vivid images of the final book of the New Testament, Revelation. It is a very complex book written to Christians to encourage them to resist the power of the Roman Empire and to be faithful, even to death, following Jesus, who is represented in the figure of a lamb. In this book judgment is described as a lake of fire. Is this destruction or purifying transformation? We have already mentioned that elsewhere in the New Testament fire is a symbol of purification. So this is at least a possible interpretation. What's more there are other indications that the prospect of an ultimately universal redemption is here also.

Firstly, we note the following universalist verses.

I heard *every creature* in heaven, and on earth, and under the earth, and in the sea, and *all* that is in them singing: "To the One seated on the throne and to the Lamb be blessing and honor and glory and might forever and ever!" (Revelation 5:13)

And the one who was seated on the throne said, "See, I am making *all things* new." (Revelation 21:5)

Secondly, it is important to note that although the final scene of the book has an image of a heavenly city coming to earth, and although there are those outside this city who because of their condition do not enter the city, it is clearly implied that although this is the end of the book it is not the end of the story. We are told of this city that:

Its gates will never be shut by day and there will be no night there. (Revelation 21:25)

What's more, the final chorus before John of Patmos signs off is an open invitation not a final closure.

The Spirit and the bride say "Come."

Let everyone who hears say "Come."

And let everyone who is thirsty come.

Let everyone who wishes take the water of life as a gift. (Revelation 22:17)

For a fuller account of this issue you can read this article by Brad Jersak entitled "Permit Me to Hope."[5]

---

5. https://afkimel.wordpress.com/2015/12/07/permit-me-to-hope/.

4

Those Questions Again —Conclusions

In the light of what we have said so far, how would we now answer the questions with which we began?

So if Christianity is about "following Jesus":

- Who is Jesus?
- Why follow anyone in the first place? Isn't it better to be a leader than a follower?
- What's involved in following Jesus rather than just being interested in him?

As for the Spirit of God empowering us:

- What is the Spirit? Is it just another name for God or something different?
- Why do we need power? Can't we just do it ourselves?
- Is this some kind of "superpower"?
- What does the Spirit of God do?

As if my life depends on it:

- Isn't that a bit heavy?
- Why should our life depend on anything other than physical laws?
- What does my life depend on?

- Is it *only* my life that depends on this or do the lives of other people or creatures?

- What happens to me if I don't follow Jesus? If my life depends on it, will I die if I don't?

This book has contended that the Christian life—the life introduced to us by the God Revolution—is quite different from the one most of us know. Its freedom is not the arbitrary freedom to make "choices" in a meaningless universe, which condemns me to create my own meaning out of nothing. The Christian life is not only dependent on the constant dynamic action of God but is in different ways dependent on a multifaceted world that is rich in texture, meaningful on multiple levels, and that cannot be explained by any one science like biology or physics. It is a life lived in response to and dependence on God in God's world, where truth, beauty, and goodness, although we only see them through a glass darkly, nevertheless have a proper place. It is also a life lived hopefully in spite of suffering and evil. All of this and more is what it means to affirm that our true flourishing as a human being is in a place of dependence on God—the creator whom Jesus called Abba.

Those who follow Jesus assume that he is the first and only fully human person in a world where human beings are enmeshed in practices in which we destroy each other and the non-human world around us. He lived life in absolute dependence on his Abba and so could give himself in total love for those around him. The resurrection of Jesus is the decisive moment for Christian faith. It means simply that God has lived our life among us; God has vindicated Jesus and is intimately involved with us and our future. "Christ" is not a surname. It is the Greek word meaning Messiah. It means that we see in him the arrival of God's justice in our lives and commit ourselves to sharing in that same life. Justice just means the right way to live. In the life of Jesus God shows us the right way to live. The Christian experience of Jesus is not merely one of being instructed by God but also one of being embraced, forgiven and empowered by God to share in his life.

This new life comes to us firstly as a gift and then as a summons. As the Spirit opens our defensive and anxious lives to the life of God our experience is akin to that of the resurrection experience of those first disciples. We know ourselves to be living in such a deep contrast to the life of Jesus. We know our solidarity in sin with those who killed Jesus. Simultaneously we know ourselves to be embraced by God's welcome. We know there is no going back and our life begins again, this time in the conscious presence of God and of Jesus Christ.

The power of the Spirit is not a superpower if by that we mean an ability to live outside the normal parameters of creation and do things like fly through the air and lift large buildings. Rather the spirit empowers us to participate in the life of Jesus—in the God Revolution. It is not an insurance scheme against suffering. On the contrary, it is a way of learning to suffer and live in the shadow of death in the confidence that death no longer has power over us! It is the transformation of our normally anxious and fearful powers so they are reshaped anew in the power of love. This power and this knowledge will have its special moments; however, for the most part the Christian life and experience is a slow transformation of the mind and heart. It is a life of freedom and patience growing in the hope of the resurrection. It is an experiment in sharing our life with others who are Jesus's followers—God revolutionaries. The best is yet to come. God is searching us all out. Now is the time to let go and live.

Where To from Here?

Here are some suggestions:

Prayer: Forget about words for a moment, take a deep breath and silence yourself before God and listen with all of your being. This is the heart of prayer. God's absence is not a hindrance to prayer. God is not absent. Our minds are cluttered in a constant internal chatter. The beauty of God's creativity and the life of Jesus is there to be seen in the most surprising places. Pray in silence. Pray with your eyes open. Listen before you speak or ask.

And as you listen you will learn to desire what is God's own desire for you and for those you meet.

Prayer is the coming together of listening and asking in the presence of God. If you want to have your desires shaped by the God Revolution you might like to pray according to Jesus's own template for prayer (Matthew 6:9–13). The "Lord's Prayer" gives us a template of what Jesus desired of God. It teaches us desire.

Community: Find a community that seeks to practice justice. Not simply a community with a strong moral agenda, but a community whose vision and life looks something like the justice of God we see in Jesus of Nazareth. Whether the community calls itself Church is not the important thing. Practices of attention to the life, death, and resurrection of Jesus and a pervasive sense of gratitude and of our ongoing need of God are much more important.

Mission: God's mission to redeem the human community and with it the whole creation in which we live is constantly on the move. To find a meaningful life in this context is never something I find for my own sake. It is to be "sent" out to a broken world as Christ was sent to a broken world. The life of the Christian community should be constantly moving out beyond any boundaries and infecting the wider society, expecting to find the Spirit of God at work there also.

Bibliography

Bauckham, Richard. *Jesus and the God of Israel*. Milton Keynes: Paternoster, 2008.

Cornford, Jonathan. *Coming Back to Earth: Essays on the Church, Climate Change, Cities, Agriculture and Eating*. Northcote, Vic, Australia: Morning Star, 2016.

Dawkins, Richard. *The Selfish Gene*. Oxford: Oxford University Press, 1976.

Dozeman, Thomas B. And Schmid, Conrad. *Farewell to the Yahwist?: The Composition of the Pentateuch in Recent European Interpretation*. Society of Biblical Literature Symposium Series, 34, 2006.

Einstein, Albert. "Physics and Reality" (1936), 59–97. In *Out of my Later Years*. New York: Carol Group, 1995.

Fabricius, Kim. "Out of Nothing God Created" in *Paddling by the Shore: Hymns of Kim Fabricius*, 10. Eugene, Or, Wipf and Stock, 2015.

Francis, Pope. *Laudato Si: On Care for our Common Home*. *http://w2.vatican. va/content/francesco/en/encyclicals/documents/papa-francesco_20150524_ enciclica-laudato-si.pdf*.

Girard, René. *I See Satan Fall Like Lightning*. Maryknoll: Orbis, 2001.

Hardin, Michael. *The Jesus Driven Life: Reconnecting Humanity with Jesus*. Lancaster, PA: JDL, 2010.

Hart, David Bentley. "Seeing the God." *First Things*, on The Back Page (February 2013). https://www.firstthings.com/article/2013/02/seeing-the-god.

Heim, Mark *Saved from Sacrifice: A Theology of the Cross*. Grand Rapids: Eerdmans, 2006.

Jenson, Robert. *Systematic Theology*, Volume 1. Oxford: Oxford University Press, 1999.

Jersak, Brad. "Permit Me to Hope." https://afkimel.wordpress.com/2015/12/07/ permit-me-to-hope/.

Johnson, Crockett. *Harold and the Purple Crayon*. USA: HarperCollins, 1955.

McCabe, Herbert. *God Still Matters*. Edited by Brian Davies. New York: Continuum, 2002.

Rapien, Alvin Yalong. "The High Priest as Representative Angel and God Incarnate (Creation Temple and Atonement: part 3)." http://www.thepoorinspirit.com/post/132892154401/the-high-priest-as-representative-angel-and-god.

Sacks, Jonathan. *Not in God's Name: Confronting Religious Violence.* London: Hodder and Stoughton, 2015.

Williams, Rowan. *Meeting God in Paul.* London: SPCK, 2015.

Lightning Source UK Ltd.
Milton Keynes UK
UKHW01f0637250918
329480UK00002B/600/P